MI...

TOUR...

WITH MAP

LA MADUNINA

PIANTE e GUIDE

EDIZIONI **DI LAURO** MILANO

20155 - VIA GOVONE G. 51 - TELEFONO 31.22.58 - 34.75.70

GUIDA DEPOSITATA A NORMA DI LEGGE
RIPRODUZIONE VIETATA

Testi del Cav. Raimondo Aresi
Pianta topografica: Edizione Di Lauro
Foto: Negri - Trezzano S/N (Milano)
Stampa: Arti Grafiche Negri - Trezzano S/N (Milano)

**THE STREETS TO RUN ALONG IN ORATER
TO VISIT THE FOLLOWING MONUMENTS
FROM P.ZA DEL DUOMO
WITH REFERENCE TO THE MAP.**

1 **The Cathedral**

2 **Cathedral Square** (starting point to all directions)

3 **Galleria Vittorio Emanuele II** (on the left side of
   Cathedral Square)

4 **P.za Mercanti, Palazzo della Ragione, Loggia degli
   Osii** (in front of the Cathedral Square on the left
   side of via Mercanti)

5 **Scala Square.** Via Mengoni, via S. Margherita

6 **San Fedele Square.** Via Mengoni, via S. Margherita,
   p.za Scala, via Marino, p.za San Fedele

7 **The « Casa degli Omenoni », Manzoni's House, Poldi
   Pezzoli Museum.** Via Mengoni, p.za Scala, via Case
   Rotte

8 **The Basilica of St. Carlo** (p.za San Carlo). On the
   left side of c.so Vitt. Emanuele

9 **The Church of St. Babila, Seminario Maggiore.** S.
   Babila - c.so Venezia 11, p.za Duomo, c.so Vitt. Emanuele, p.za San Babila

10 **The public gardens, the Natural History Museum,
   the Planetary** (c.so Venezia). C.so Vitt. Emanuele,
   p.za San Babila, c.so Venezia, via Palestro

11 **Villa Reale, Modern Art Gallery** (via Palestro). C.so
   Vitt. Emanuele, c.so Venezia, via Palestro

12 **The Brera Picture-Gallery** (via Brera). Via Mengoni,
   p.za Scala, via Verdi, via Brera

13 **St. Mark's Church** (p.za San Marco). Via Mengoni,
   via Manzoni, p.za Cavour, via Fatebenefratelli

14 **St. Simpliciano Basilica Virginum** (p.za San Simpliciano). Via Mercanti, via Broletto, via Mercato, on
   the right side of c.so Garibaldi

15 **The Sforzesco Castle** (p.za Castello). Via Mercanti, via Dante, l.go Cairoli, p.za Castello

16 **The Monumental Cemetery** (p.za Cimitero Monumentale). Via Mercanti, via Dante, Foro Buonaparte, via Legnano, via Montello, at the end of via Ceresio.

17 **The Arc of Peace** (p.za Sempione). Via Mercanti, via Dante, Foro Buonaparte, parco Sempione

18 **The Church of Santa Maria delle Grazie** (p.za S. M. delle Grazie). Via Mercanti, via Meravigli, on the right side of c.so Magenta

19 **Da Vinci's « Last Supper ».** The some as above

20 **The Museum of Science and Technology** (via San Vittore). Via Mercanti, via Meravigli, c.so Magenta, via S. Agnese, p.za S. Ambrogio, via San Vittore

21 **The Basilica of St. Ambrogio** (p.za S. Ambrogio). Via Mercanti, via Meravigli, c.so Magenta, via S. Agnese, p.za S. Ambrogio

22 **San Maurizio al Monastero Maggiore, The Archeological Museum, Palazzo Litta** (c.so Magenta 24). Via Mercanti, via Meravigli, c.so Magenta 24

23 **The Ambrosian Library and its Art Gallery** (p.za Pio XI). Via Orefici, via Cantú, p.za Pio XI

24 **Santa Maria presso San Satiro** (via Torino). On the left side of via Torino 19

25 **St. Alexander's Church, the Arcimbolde Schools, the Trivulzio Building** (p.za Sant'Alessandro). On the left side of via Torino, at the end of via Palla, p.za S. Alessandro

26 **The Basilica of St. Lorenzo Maggiore** (c.so Ticinese. 37). Via Torino, al Carrobbio, on the left side of c.so Ticinese

27 **The Basilica of St. Eustorgio** (p.za S. Eustorgio). Via Torino, al Carrobbio, at the end of c.so Ticinese

28 **The Sanctuary of St. Maria and the Church of St. Celso** (c.so Italia). Via Mazzini, p.za Missori, on the left side of c.so Italia

29 **San Nazaro in Brolo's** (p.za San Nazaro). Via Mazzini, p.za Missori, on the left side of c.so Porta Romana

30 **The Main Hospital** (p.za Festa del Perdono). Via Arcivescovado, p.za Fontana, p.za Santo Stefano, on the right side of via Laghetto

31 **St. Maria della Passione's** (via della Passione). C.so Vitt. Emanuele, p.za S. Babila, via Borgogna, via Mascagni, via Conservatorio

32 **St. Maria alla Fontana** (p.za S. M. alla Fontana). Via Mercanti, via Dante, Foro Buonaparte, via Legnano, via Montello, on the right side of via Farini

33 **The Charterhouse of Garegnano** (via Garegnano). Via Mercanti, via Dante, Foro Buonaparte, parco Sempione, c.so Sempione, at the end on the left side of v.le Certosa

34 **The Charterhouse of Chiaravalle** (via S. Arialdo 102). Via Mazzini, p.za Missori, c.so Lodi, p.le Corvetto, Rogoredo, Chiaravalle

35 **The Abbey of Viboldone** (via Emilia). Via Mazzini, p.za Missori, c.so P.ta Romana, c.so Lodi, p.le Corvetto, Rogoredo, via Emilia, San Giuliano

36 **The Abbey of Mirasole** (per via Ripamonti). Via Mazzini, p.za Missori, c.so P.ta Romana, c.so Vigentina, via Ripamonti, Quintosole, Noverasco

37 **The Charterhouse of Pavia** (strada per Pavia km. 27 da Milano). Via Torino, c.so Ticinese, c.so San Gottardo, via Torricelli, via A. Sforza, on the left side of via Chiesa Rossa, at 27th km.

A historical outline of Milan

Milan is an important centre whose main activities are industry, trade and finance. It covers a total area of 182 square kilometers and has an establishished population of over one million nine hundred thousand. The earliest history of Milan dates back to 400 B.C. with the settling of Gallic tribes in the heart of the Po Valley. These tribes mixed with the already existing Insubres, and the Etruscans, whose splendid historical era was about to close. Both the age of foundation and the origin of its name are derived from tradition. Historians base their theories on archeological findings which have been dug up from Milan's sub-soil. The ancient name " Mediolanium " might have its origin in the settling of Belloveso and his tribes in the centre of the Plain of Lombardy, that is in the centre of the triangle between the rivers Po, Ticino and Adda. Legend has it that the name is derived from the " scrofa semi lanuta ", that is half-woollen sow, (from the Latin: medio = semi and lanum = wool), but this seems improbable although the sow may have been used in the coat-of-arms. In 222 B.C. the Romans invaded Milan and development has been going on ever since. The once small village grew larger and greater, and out of the original few acres of the early " Castrum " it reached the peak of its splendor in the third and fourth centuries. The poet Ausonio called it " Roma secunda " (the second Rome). Massimiano, who shared the empire with Diocleziano, established his residence here, and undertook to embellish it with great new buildings and wider walls. In 313 Constantine proclaimed his famous edict of free worship, here in Milan. In this period the paleochristian basilicas were built. In 374 St. Ambrose was appointed bishop of the diocese, and on his death, in 397, the Milanese Church took up the Ambrosian Rite which is still used today. The most admired and remarkable remains of the Roman " Mediolanum " are the sixteen columns of St. Lorenzo in Corso Ticinese, while the Massimiano walls are partly incorporated into the Archeological Museum, this is found in Corso Magenta. Other valuable archeological remains are to be found in the basements of houses in the historical centre of the city. The barbaric raiders who invaded Italy during the course of the centuries, passed through Milan, plundering and destroying as they did so. The last destruction which it suffered were the 1943 bombing raids. From the ruins of Milan was built a greater and more industrial city, this was due to its talented and strong willed population. Milan was not the Longobard capital although it was the residence of Duke Albino, who had taken up court at the " Curia Ducis " where Cordusio now stands, in fact the name of the square is derived from this court. Charlemagne, king of the Franks, succeeded to the Longobard domination, but very few signs of this domination remain; a few ruins of the " Regio Ducale Palazzo " — also know as Arengo — remain of the Comunal period, these are incorporated into the Royal Palace, and the " Palazzo della Ragione " in Piazza Mercanti which was the commercial heart of medieval Milan. The various stages of Milan's history are bound up to the development of the city. From the time of the shortlived Torrianis period, to the Viscontis, to the Sforzas under Ludovico the Moor, right up to the sixteenth century when Milan was the heart of humanistic studies, and the Lombardic artistic Renaissance was at its height. After the fall of the Sforzas, Milan fell under French, then Spanish and finally, under Austrian domination. Under the rule of Mary Teresa of Austria, thanks to the stimulation of the Illuminists of Milan such as Beccaria, Verri and others, the organization of public administration became possible, this was done by creating the cadastre. Then followed the Cisalpina Republic, followed by Napoleon's Italian Republic, and after the fall of Napoleon the

Austrians returned. The year 1848, with its fatidical " Five Days ", brought to Milan a short-lived moment of freedom which was to be followed by the worst period of Austrian domination. Only in 1859 did Milan and Lombardy cease to be under the domination of some foreign power. Milan was, by that time, the capital city of a kingdom, but it ceased to be independent and entered the nation as a city, to become an ever developing part of it.

1 The Cathedral

The building in a decorative-Gothic style, was begun in 1386. The ruler of Milan, Gian Galeazzo Visconti, placed the Candoglia mountain, from which to excavate the necessary marble, at the disposition of the people. The cathedral is the work of brilliant artists, architects, engineers and sculptors besides a host of anonymous other workers. It is an ornamental aereal work in pinkish marble, which after six centuries of existence is still not yet really finished owing to the fact that it is continually subject to maitenance and restoration work. It is rich in external decoration, with statues and alto-rilievo work and crowned by 135 towering spires, on the highest of which stands the " Madonnina ". The interior, like the exterior, is decorated with statues, alto-rilievo work, decorations and valuable works of art; the stained glass windows are of particular artistic interest. The facade, like the rest of the building, gives the impression of belonging to one single style, although the influence of various periods are distinguishable. It was begun in a neo-classical style by Pelligrino Pelligrini, known as Tibaldi, but remained unfinished for a long time; it was only during the first years of the nineteenth century that definite completion work was begun. The five portals and their respective windows were utilized, so giving a hybrid façade. The five bronze doors, begun during the early years of this century, were completed in 1965 and are the masterpieces of different artists. In front of the facade, is the built Antiquarium, to preserve the remains of the baptistery of St. John, which once existed between the basilicas of St. Tecla and St. Maria Maggiore; it is the most ancient baptistery in Milan and is an octogonal building built before St. Ambrose's, sometime between 378 and 386. Here, during the night between the 24th. and the 25th. of April 378, St. Ambrose baptized St. Augustine.

2 The Cathedral square and the Royal Palace

The arrangement of the square in front of the cathedral, as we see it today, was planned by the architect Giuseppe Mengoni who gave a new organic appearance to it by building the archway which opens onto the " Galleria ". In the centre of the square can be seen the monument to Victor Emanuel II (1896), a work in bronze done by Ercole Rosa. On the north portico side of the square, under the square itself, the underground station has been built. Between this station and the one in Piazza Cordusio a pedestrian subway has been built which links Piazza Cordusio with Corso Vittorio Emanuele. During the excavations for this work, archeological remains came to light, especially those of the ancient basilica of St. Tecla, today are preserved, partly in the Antiquarium of the Baptistery, and partly in an adjacent building. To the right of the cathedral can be seen the Royal Palace. Built in 1145 under the name of " Broletto dei Consoli ", it was later destroyed by Barbarossa, and then rebuilt, later to become the seat of the main public offices. After the fall of the Torrianis the palace became the home of the Visconti family, and later of the Sforzas who, however, soon moved to their favourite residence, the Castle. Towards the end of the eighteenth century the palace was subjected to radical transformation by the architect Giuseppe Piermarini. Bomb damage during the last war destroyed nearly all the rooms of the royal apartment and consequently, frescoes, as well as, valuable stuccoes and other decorations were destroyed too. The rich neo-classical furniture was however, saved. The hall of Caryatids, the largest in Milan, badly, but not unrepairably, damaged is evidence of its ancient beauty. The second floor, houses art exhibitions organized by the "Ente Manifestazioni Milanesi". Inside the "Regio Ducal Palazzo" is to be found the church of St. Gottardo built in 1336.

3 The " Vittorio Emanuele " gallery

The gallery dedicated to Victor Emanuel is an impressive arcade, a typical example of the eclectic architecture which flourished after the Italian Risorgimento. Many houses and buildings were demolished between Piazza del Duomo and Piazza della Scala in order to make room for it. The first stone was laid in the centre of the octagon on March 7th. 1865 in the king's presence. Two years later, although it was still unfinished, the gallery was opened to the public. The architect Mengoni's work was finished in 1877 when the entrance archway was completed. The day before the inauguration ceremony, Mengoni climbed up onto the scaffolding, and standing on a plank which gave way, plunged to his death. The gallery is in the form of a cross, its major wing is 195 meters long, the minor one being 105 meters. Above the centre of the octagon there is a dome rising to the height of 50 meters above ground level, owing to the fact that it is built in glass and iron, like the rest of the roof, it is known as " the glass sky ". The composition symbolizes the four parts of the world, these were originally painted by Petrasanta, Giuliano, Pagliano and Casnedi in the lunettes of the octagon, but were replaced in 1910 with mosaic reproductions. The gallery suffered serious bomb damage in 1943, and it took many years to put it right again. In 1967, when the ground-work was finally finished, the restoration could be declared finished. Brightly illuminated shops of all kinds and restaurants give it a distinguished appearance, so much so as to give it its nick-name of " Milan's sitting room ". Centre of all political and civic manifestations in Milan, its coffee-houses have always been the meeting places of artists, scholars and politicians. The gallery has also been the meeting place of musicians and opera singers. The Galleria is the heart of the Milan, it is the finest covered arcade in Italy, perhaps even the finest in Europe.

4 Piazza Mercanti - Palazzo della Ragione - Loggia degli Osii

Piazza dei Mercanti (the Merchants' Square) wa originally, closed in. Now it is bounded by Palaz della Ragione (House of Reason), and the Logg of the Osii, the Palatine Schools and the Panig rolas' House. Via dei Mercanti runs between F lazzo della Ragione and the " Juriconsults' Bu ding " thus linking Piazza del Duomo to Cordusi The Mayor Oldrado da Tresseno had the Hou of Reason built in 1233, and his effigy, in al rilievo, can be seen in front of the building. It w given the name of " New Broletto " as the new on already existed on the site of the present-da Royal Palace. It is built in brick and stone, the ground floor there is an open portico, whi the upper floor contains a large hall. Another flo was added to the building in 1773 to contain t notorial archives, nowadays housed in a differe building. Plans are being made to demolish th ugly added floor, thus giving the building i original medieval appearance.

The Loggia of the Osii was built by Matteo Viscor in 1316. It was restored in 1904 and the deform ations of the XVIIth. and XVIIIth. centuries we removed. The façade, with two superimpose loggias, is built in black and white marble. the centre of the upper loggia there is a balcor commonly known as the " Parléra ", on which ca be seen the heraldic signs of the various quarte of Milan, plus the Viscontis' coat-of-arms. On t other loggis, in niches especially built for the are statues of Milanese saints, the work of Car pionese and Comoese artists. On one side of t Loggia of the Osii stands the building of t Palatine Schools. The façade is the work Seregni, who followed the lines of the Juriconsul Building. At the top of the great staircase, the is a bronze bust of C. M. Maggi, a poet who wro in Italian and the Vernacular Milanese dialed

5 The Scala Theatre and square

The Scala Theatre was built between 1776 and 1778 on the site of the church of St. Maria alla Scala from which it takes its name. The work of the architect Giuseppe Piermarini, it was inaugurated on August 3rd. 1778 with the lyrical opera " L'Europa Riconosciuta " by Antonio Salieri. Built in a neoclassical style, the face has a covered portico and a gable with an alto-rilievo work representing " Apollo's Chariot ". The building suffered severe bomb damage in 1943, but was re-built without any alteration to its characteristic features, and was re-opened to the public in 1946 with a concert given by Arturo Toscanini. Adjacent to the theatre is the Theatrical Museum.. The plentiful material on display is a documental collection of the evolution of theatrical costumes from the period of Ancient Greece up to the classical theatrical period. Various objects on show also belong to the modern and contemporary evolution of the theatre. In 1952 the museum was endowed with Renato Simoni's legacy, this includes a large collection of objects pertaining to the theatre and over 37,000 books. The legacy is registered under the name of Livia Simoni, that is Renato's mother. The " Fondo Cornia " has recently donated to the theatre a collection of some 600 recordings of the voices of famous opera singers who performed between the end of the nineteenth century and the beginning of the twentieth.

In Piazza della Scala, the most impressive thing, after the front of the theatre, is the façade of Palazzo Marino, this was built in 1890 by Luca Alessi. Palazzo Marino has been the seat of the city council since 1890. Reconstructed after the war, it is ne of the finest buildings in Milan. In the centre of the square is the monument Pietro Magni built in 1872 to Leonardo da Vinci, this is surrounded by his favourite followers A. Salaino, G. A. Boltraffio, C. da Sesto and M. d'Oggiono.

6 The square and the church of St. Fedele

The St. Fedele square is a regular quadrilateral, on one side of which stands the church of St. Fedele, and on the other Palazzo Marino, these two sides are the seats of two banks and a new building. In the square itself is the monument to Alessandro Manzoni, erected in 1883.

The name St. Fedele was given to a small church dating back to the 12th century. In 1556 St. Carlo Borromeo gave the church and the houses adjacent to it, to the Jesuits. Between 1549 and 1579 the Cardinal had Pelligrino Pelligrini, know as " il Tibaldi ", build a new church, but he left this work unfinished; nor was it completed by his successor Martino Bassi who only succeeded in completing the interior, while the apse, as it is seen today, is still unfinished in its exterior decorations. After the bomb damage the church was restored.

Palazzo Marino, whose façade looks onto Piazza St. Fedele, while the other sides look over Via Case Rotte and Via Marino, here shows the original part built according to G. Alessi's designs. The building was ordered by Tommaso Marino, a Genoese who had become rich by trading in salt, it was begun in 1553 and finished in 1558. The magnificent courtyard of honour, whose entrance is in Via Marino, is a jewel of Alessi's architecture, in it can be seen sculptural decoration, lavishly put everywhere, which is the expression of the genius of this artist from Perugia. On the ground floor a portico runs all round the four sides, while on the first floor there is a magnificent loggia. The courtyard leads to the so-called "Alessi's Hall", once used as a committee room of the city council, but now used for other ceremonies. According to scholars, in the " Green Room ", which stands on the corner of Via Case Rotte, was born Count Marino's grandchild Virginia di Leyva, the Nun of Monza, immortalized by Manzoni in his " The Betrothed ".

7 The "Casa degli Omenoni" - Manzoni's house - The Poldi Pezzoli Museum

The "House of the Omenoni" was built by Leone Leoni and is one of the most interesting late sixteenth century buildings in Milan. It has eight caryatids called "Omenoni" (big men) which are the work of Antonio Abbondio and are of Michelangelesque inspiration. Inside there is a court-yard surrounded by porticos with Tuscan columns. The façade has some fine stone decorations and below the cornice, which supports the roof, there is a fine frieze in alto-rilievo representing "Slander devoured by lions".

In Piazza Belgioioso, other than the building which gives it its name, we can see Palazzo Besana and Manzoni's house. This latter is very dear to the people of Milan as their own great poet, together with his family, lived in it for over fifty years. Now the building, together with its rich library, houses the "Centre for Manzonian Studies".

The apartment in Via Manzoni No. 12 in which the Poldi Pezzoli Museum is housed, was destined to become a museum by a member of a noble family, Gian Giacomo Poldi Pezzoli in 1878. It contains many rare pictures of the Lombardic School other than porcelains, enamels, jewels and other objects of unestimatable value. The profile of Pollaiolo's "Young Woman" has a magic atmosphere, and is an excellent example of refined Renaissance culture. The collection of ancient arms, most of which were manufactured in Milan, is very famous. It was badly damaged during the war, and as it was nothing but ruins, it was decided to definitely demolish it. But the will of Ettore Modigliani, and after his death, that of Fernanda Wittgens, succeeded in imposing its re-building on the same site. The Poldi Pezzoli Museum is the richest and best private collecting in Europe, and can compete with the Wallace collection in London and the Jaquemart in Paris.

8 The basilica of St. Carlo

The present day basilica of St. Carlo was built on the site of the old church and convent of the Servants of Mary. When preparations for Ferdinando I of Austria's entrance into Milan were being made, orders were given to demolish, the chapel of the old convent which faced the "Servants' Walk", in order to make the Imperial procession easier. Later, for the arrangement of the "walk", renamed Corso Arciduca Ferdinando, total demolition of the church was decreed. The parish priest, Giacinto Amati, proposed the building of a new church on the same site wich was to be dedicated to St. Carlo Borromeo. Don Giacinto's brother, the architect Carlo Amati was engaged to make projects. The Amati plans were widely discussed and in part revised in order to vault the ceiling. Owing to the difficulties involved in this great task, the architect Felice Pizzagalli was called in, he had already experimented his new system in other Milanese churches. It must be admitted that the cupola has been proven twice; once during the fire of 1895 and once during the 1943 bombing. The basilica is in Neo-classical style and is a free interpretation of the Pantheon with its exact dimensions. In order to adorn the church the sculptors Pompeo Marchesi and Motelli, and the painter Angelo Inganni were called in to carry out some of their precious work. In the recent adjustment of the convent the Chapel of the Pietà was abolished, and the sculptural work which was in it was taken to the church of the Addolorata at San Siro. The pronaus of the basilica is in eight monolithic columns of Baveno granite, rising above them is the wide fully curved cupola, this is situated on a high tambour beat out of columns half embedded in the wall. The solemn appearance of the architectural assembly is diminished by the excessive height of the buildings in the square around it, buildings which Amati intented to be one-storeyed.

The basilica of San Babila, now squashed in by modern buildings, was, perhaps, built at the end of the XIth century on the site of another, but older, church founded by St. Lorenzo I between 489 and 511. It is the best known romantic church in Milan. The sides, left unaltered, have buttresses alternating with arched windows with lintels, and in the octangle tiberium can be seen evident traces of romanesque structures. The interior has three naves with barrel vaults supported on mighty pillars. In the middle of the transcept rises the hemispherical cupola with an octagonal base and conical pendentives. Traces of some XIVth century frescoes still remain, there are also six of Giuseppe Mentessi's panels and the altar-piece of a chapel done by Lodovico Pogliaghi.

At No. 11 Corso Venezia we can see the building which was once the "Seminario Maggiore" founded by St. Carlo in 1561, this buildings built on the site of the ancient "Umiliati" monastery, which is, at the moment, being restored to be used as a centre for eccliastical studies. The monumental entrance, adorned with two colossal caryatids, and dominated by St. Carlo's coat-of-arms, was designed by F.M. Richini in 1652. The interior of the building has a courtyard with a colonnade and two superimposed porticos, architraves with granite columns which recall a certain palladian influence.

At No. 10 Corso Venezia is the Fontana houses better known as the Silvestri house; this is the oldest building in the street, beautified by the grace of Lombardic Renaissance work in which can be seen Bramante's influence. Having suffered bomb damage it was restored between 1959 and 1962. This building is a typical squire's manor. It has windows with brick lintels and a fine marble doorway with candelabrum columns. Inside there is a colonnade on three sides with an elegant portico.

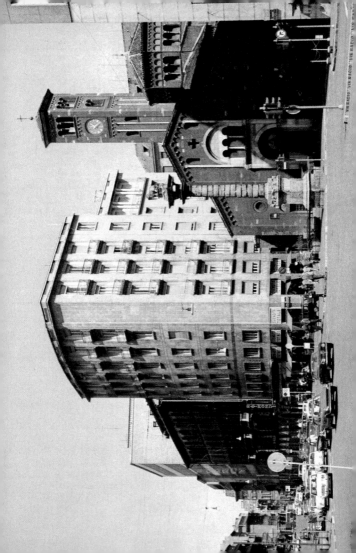

10 The public gardens - The Natural History Museum - The Planetary

The public gardens cover an area of about forty two acres. The gardens were orignally laid out by Piermarini in 1782, but the architect Giuseppe Balzaretti, in 1858, and finally in 1881 Alemagna laid them as we see them today. The gardens of the Dugnani Palace are part of them, this building constructed in 1600, was the first seat of the Natural History Museum; the main hall of this building was beautifully decorated with the fresco paintings done by G.B. Tiepolo in 1731.

The Natural History Museum was founded in 1838 by incorporating the Giuseppe De Cristoforis and Giorgio Jan collections; its original seat, as we have already said, was in the Dugnani Palace. The present day building dates back to 1839. This building was also damaged during the wear and its restoration was a very slow job. Of the twenty three halls only about fifteen are open. The museum contains department of minerals, rock, fossils and animals. The museum also has a specialized library.

The Planetary is in Corso Venezia built against the suggestive background of the public gardens, it was given to the city, his adoptive home, by the editor Ulrico Hoepli in 1930. It is considered one of the most interesting institutes of culture and popular education in Milan. Conferences, at which are projected films of the principle celestial phenomena, are held there. It has a seating capacity of 250 to 300 places with rotable seats with flexible back rests so as to allow the viewer to follow the speaker's indications of the celestial vault, this is reproduced by a perfect instrument onto the cupola whose inferior limit reproduces the complete horizon of the city. The Planetary has a library containing works on astronomy, the majority of which are illustrated astronomical atlases.

11 Villa Reale and the Modern Art Gallery

This building is commonly called the "Royal Villa"
but it was built by the Viennese architecht Leopold
Pollak in 1790 as the home of Count Lodovico Bar-
biano di Belgioioso. The entrance opens onto Via
Palestro overlooking the public gardens, but the
main façade is the one which overlooks the "Eng-
lish" garden with its rock gardens and little lake.
The architecture acquires a particualr grace through
the harmonious equilibrium of its element. The
villa was bought in 1803 by the Cisalpina Republic
and given to Napoleon who lived there with his
wife Josephine. Also his step-son Eugene de Bea-
harneais, viceroy of the Italian Kingdom, lived
there. Later, the Austrian Marshal Radetzky died
there. In 1859 it passed into the hands of the Savoy
family, and 1919 it became the property of the City
of Milan. Since 1921 it has housed the Modern Art
Gallery, originally housed in the Sforzesco Castle.
After the repairs following the wartime bomb
damage, it was once more opened as an art gallery.
In 1955 a new department of contemporary art
was added. The furnishing, rich in neo-classical
furniture, giver the rooms an aristocratic air. In
the great hall, the "Apollo citharist surrounded by
the muses" painted on the vaulted ceiling by Andrea
Appiani in 1811, is one of the best works of this
neo-classical artist.

The museum contains nineteenth century works of
art from Francesco Havez to Tranguillo Cremona,
it contains his celebrated "Falconiere" (Falconer);
Giovanni Segantini's "Le due madri" (The two
mothers); Mosè Bianchi's "Traversata in Laguna"
(Crossing the Lagoon); Domenico Induno's "La
scuola delle sartine" (School for dressmakers); Gaetano Previati's "La Madonna dei gigli" (the Madonna of the lilies) and manv others. Among the
scultputer Medardo Rossi's wax statues stand out,
among these we can see the expressive "Portinaia"
(door-keeper) which is an excellent example.

The name Brera come from the place where the "Umiliati" (an order of religious men and laymen) built their house within the city walls in about 1170. In the XIIIth century the church of St. Mary of Brera was added to the convent, this was built by Giovanni di Balduccio of Pisa and adorned by artists from Como. When the "Umiliati" period fell, the Jesuites succeeded them, and 1772, when this order was suspended, Mary Teresa of Austria destined the building to be the seat of an institute of science, letters and arts. The first part of the artistic collection was founded by the Abbot Giuseppe Bianconi who became secretary of the new Academy of Fine Arts in 1775. The gallery was really begun during the full splendor of the Napoleonic period on the wish of Bonapart himself. It was started by gathering together works from Religious orders, churches and convents which had been suspended during the Cisalpina Republic, and was inaugurated on August 15th. 1809. During the nineteenth century it was enriched by private legacies and donations, and after the first world war it was enlarged, but, when it seemed to have taken on its final form, war broke out, and, in 1940 bombing made the moving of all the works to a safe place, necessary. On June 9th. 1950 the gallery was reopened, a brighter and more beautiful place, from the "Little Brera" appeared the "Great Brera". The artistic works range from the 14th. century, with Ambrogio Lorenzetti's "Madonna" to nineteenth and twentieth century ones, with the works of Lombardic and Ventian schools and a few Florentine ones. Among the most noteworthy works are Mocchirolo's "Oratorio", reproduced here, with frescoes by Giovanni da Milano. Raffaelio's well known "Sposalizio della Vergine"; Mantegna's "Cristo Morto"; Bramante's "Cristo alla Colonna". Among the modern artists works by Hayez, Fattori, Segantini, Zandomeneghi and Boccioni.

RAFFAELLO SANZIO
Sposalizio della Vergine

It is to be seen in St. Mark's square on the corner of Via Fatebenefratelli. It was founded by Lanfranco da Settala (1264), whose fine tombal monument, work of the XVth. century Campionese School, is to be found inside the church. The façade is the result of the completion work carried out in 1872, by the architect Maciachini who intended to take up again the idea of one of Matteo da Campione's pupils (belonging to the end of the XIVth. and early XVth centuries). He left the doorway, Menclozzo's architecture, and the statue of St. Mark standing between those of St. Ambrose and St. Augustine seen above the doorway, these are the work of the Campione master known as Viboldone, but he added the pinnacles to underline the Gothic. The bell tower as added at the same time, dating back to the first decade of the XIV century and was completed by Mongeri with a portico and spire. The idea that the bell tower was the one cut off by the governor Ferrante Gonzaga was unfounded, this was supposed to have happened in 1585 because it was higher than the bastioned enclosure built around the castle. The interior with its baroque superstructure of 1964, leaves unaltered the Latin cross shaped plan which is the outcome of the insertion of the three Gothic naves into the original structure which is Romanesque. The church is adorned with the fresco paintings of the Fiammenghini. Restoration of some parts of the church is recent, and so is the salvage of some XIVth. century fresco paintings, restored and recupered, now placed in the right transcept where, everything belonging to the romanesque construction is collected. Beside the church we can see the cloisters which were part of the Augustian monastery. It should also be remembered that on May 22nd. 1874, on the anniversary of Manzoni's death, the "Mass of Requiem" which G. Verdi had written for his friend was celebrated in the basilica of St. Mark.

14 St. Simpliciano's Basilica Virginum

St. Simpliciano's, with its large coenobium, is the most ancient and important of the three palaeochristian churches which rise in the street from Ponte Vetero to the Ramparts at Porta Comasina. This basilica was built on a graveyard ground, the first house of prayer of which would have been transformed into a church in the times of St. Ambrogio. According to the tradition, Simpliciano, his successor, laid there St. Sisino, St. Martirio and St. Alessandro corpses. The original church was dedicated to the Virgin Mary and the saint virgins, but after Simpliciano's death it took his name. Probably the church was still being built in the Longobard age, as a brick with Agilulfo seal has been found there (590-615). It was also the first church outside the walls to be visited in the Rogations day. In 881 il was St. Protaso Ad Monachos Cluniac Benedictines' see. The basilica was reconstructed in various periods; the present Lombard architectural structure dates back to the XII century. Originally, the front was hutshaped and it seems that in the past there was in front of it a four-porch-arcade similar to St. Ambrogio's. Both the apse and the « Tiburio » date back to 1170. The apse vault fresco representing « The Virgin's crowning » was painted by Bergognone. In 1600 and 1700 the basilica was damaged and its pure Romanesque lines were disfigured In 1841 the interior was covered by a bad colourless fillet plaster. Excavations and researches carried out by Prof. Edoardo Arslan after the war broght to light the palaeo-christian basilica walls. Besides the basilica, St. Simpliciano's monument includes also two cloisters: the smaller one, dating back to the XV century is very simple; the larger one, built in 1517 by Seregni, feels the effect of Alessi's influence. The monastery belonged firstly to the Cluniac Benedictines and then to the Cassineses. At present the cloisters have been restored and are fully efficient.

15 The Sforzesco Castle and its art collections

What we see today is only a part of the original citadel which, at the beginning, consisted of other forts enclosed in a great star-shaped ramparted fortress. The perimetral development of the present quadrilateral, however, makes it Italy's largest castle, and its construction would be the most beautiful of its kind had it not been subject to the injustice of time and men. But, even as it stands today, it is a majestic work, which hides behind its walls, extremely interesting Gothic-Renaissance halls and courtyards. The castle was rebuilt in 1450 by Francesco Sforza on the ruins of the viscounty fort, which, in its turn, had been built on the ruins of the Porta Giovia castle which had been knocked down by the people during the " Golden Ambrosian Republic ". Under the rule of Lodovico Maria Sforza, known as the " Moor " (1495), the castle became one of the most important royal palaces, and the best known artists and architects of the time worked on it, among others Bramante and the great master Leonardo. On the death of Francesco II, the last of the Sforzas, its regal period came to an end and it became no more than a fortress. During the Spanish, French and Austrian dominations it was used as military barracks and underwent so much damage and rough treatment that it could only be considered little more than a ruin. During the Napoleonic period a radical transformation was planned, so radical as to make it unrecognizable, and in 1859, with the defeat of the Austrians, it was used again as military barracks for the garrison troops. In 1890, when the troops were evacuated, it was decided to restore it, the job being given to the architect Luca Beltrami, who gave so much towards the saving of this famous monument. In 1893 the military authorities handed over the castle to the City, and so the transformation of the gloomy barracks into the present magnificent building,

could be begun. The castle was victim of more great damage during the bombing of 1943, but after the war more reconstruction work was done on the buildings, the Ancient Arts Museum and the halls of the forts. The front of the castle with its round towers on each side, faces the city, in the centre of the front we can see the Tower of Filarete, rebuilt in 1900 with Beltrami's refacing. The interior is divided into the great courtyard or military square, and, looking towards the park, the fort on the left, and the ducal courtyard on the right. Between these two, rises the tower added by Bona of Savoy in 1477. The two massive towers on the park-side corners give it the appearance of a fortress. The north tower houses the Hall of Assi (boards), while the other, called the Castellano Tower or Treasure Hall, contains the remains of Bramante's fresco painting of Argus.

The Ancient Arts Museum contains varied artistic material, and is interesting to visitors also for its Renaissance period halls. It is world famous for its works by Leonardo and Michelangelo, the greatest artists Italy ever produced. The museum winds through the halls on the ground and first floors of the ducal courtyard, from the Chancellery Hall one can walk along the battlements, through the tower of Bona of Savoy to the fortress hall which houses a collection of ceramics and musical instruments. In the hall once called the Scarlioni Hall because of its decorations, we find the " Pietà Rondanini ", Michelangelo's last — unfinished — work. Among the other sculptures can be seen the lying statue of Gastone of Foix by Bambaia. In the Hall of Assi, so called because of the panelling which covers the walls, Leonardo created the most prodigious decorations which transform the vault of the ceiling into a dome of extraordinarily beautiful green leaves. One of the halls is dedicated to ancient armoury and houses armoury, halberds, shields, spears, spiked clubs and helmets, most of which were produced by Milanese armour-

ers. Other rooms are the homes of antique furniture, and the picture gallery is rich in the works of Lombardic painters. The fourteenth century frescoes in the room which is a reconstruction of a room once found in the Roccabianca Castle near Parma, are also interesting as they represent the " Story of Gualtieri and Griselda ".

From the fort courtyard one can go down into the underground archeological museum which contains some really interesting pieces. Here we can find a documentation of the ruin and reconstruction of the castle itself.

Since 1902 the ground floor rooms of the fort have housed the Historic Civic Archives. Since the war the seat has been enlarged and renewed, not only the rooms but other plants have been modernized and put in working order. The preserved documents date back to 1385 and go up to the XIXth. century, some even to 1927. The Archive also contains many Portiani documents. The Trivulzian library, bought by the city in 1935 is also attached to the Civic Archives, this contains 40,000 volumes, 1,500 manuscripts and 130 illuminated manuscripts. The Bertarelli print collection bears the name of its founder, who, by giving his precious collection donated the first and most valuable part. It is a collection of prints of all kinds, from the artistic to the most popular kind. It is the only institute of its kind in Italy which contains so much iconographical material, and writers and editors often turn to them for the illustration of books and magazines.

16 The Monumental Cemetery

An iron fence rails off the external square from the internal one, closed in by the building which flow into one another to the centre of the building built as a sepuchral shrine. In this cemetery are buried the remains of illustrious citizens, when they are not actually buried here, they are remembered with medallions, busts and tombstones. The monumental construction is 51 meters high with a wide staircase leading up to the shrine itself. The main body is attached to the wings by galleries on the ground floor, these contain burial niches, and loggias on the upper floor where the actual tombs are found. On the front of the entrance to the shrine can be seen the bronze statue of Glory, work of the sculptor Lodovico Pogliaghi, who is also responsible for the mosaic work on the doors. In the centre of he shrine can be seen he tomb of Alessandro Manzoni, this is placed on a base in alto-rilievo, work of Giannino Castiglioni. The monumental Cemetery and its buildings, in Lombardic style, is the work of the architect Carlo Maciachini, the details are freely developed with bizantine forms. The enclosure, in living rock, is scattered with small chapels erected by private people on free-style designs. The Cemetery is full of monuments and valuable works done by the best architects and sculptors of the time. Among the most note-worthy of the minieteenth and twentieth centuries we can name: Butti, Lodovico Pogliaghi, Leonardo Bisolfi, Vincenzo Vela, Alfeo Bedeschi, Messina, Manzù, Giannino Castiglioni; Adolfo Wildt is present with his long-bodied figures representing men immersed in the sleep of death with such impressive sculptural anatomy. On one side of the entrance there is a Jewish cemetery and a non-catholic one. At the end of the main avenue there is the crematorium built in 1875 with the monei left by the promoter of cremation, Alberto Keller.

17 The Arch of Peace or of Semplon

Found in the semicircular opening of Piazzale Sempione, this is a regular construction with precise height limits; the Arch of Peace rising in isolation is considered the most representative object of Lombardic neo-classicism. It was begun in 1807 on plans drawn by Luigi Cagnola to celebrate the Napoleonic victories. It has a strong agile structure notwithstanding its decorative exuberance. The archway, the ideal end to the road which Napoleon had planned to use to reach Briga, and from there to open up a speedy passage for his men and arms across the Semplon Pass. The arch consists of three barrel vaults supported by Corinthian columns on pedestals, with a trabeation and a high attic above which dominates the six bronze horses cast by Abbondio Sangiorgio, and the Winged Victory done by Giovanni Putti. On the trabeation there are the four allegorical figures of the four rivers of the Italian Republic the Po and the Ticino by Cacciatori and Marchesi's Tagliamento and Adige. On the walls are accademical bas-reliefs begun by Camillo Pacetti, Pompeo Marchesi and Benedetto Cacciatori; it was finished in the atmosphere of the Austrian restoration by Peverelli and Moglia in 1833. When Napoleon fell all the figures were made unrecognizable by the addition of Roman togas. The Napoleonic arch become the symbol of the Hapsburgian peace. After the fall of Napoleon the arch was inaugurated on September 10th. 1838 with the coming of Ferdinand II of Austria to Milan to receive the "Iron Crown". Il 1859 the Arch of Peace celebrated the new national victory and under it, in solemn procesion, passed Napoleon III and Victor Emanuel II on their way into the city after the victory of the battle of Magenta; a historical fact which was repeated, a hundred years later, when to celebrate the centenary of the event, General De Gaulle and Giovanni Gronchi passed under it.

18 The church of Santa Maria delle Grazie

This church was built under the dukedom of Francesco Sforza on ground given to the Domenican monks by Count Giuseppe Vimercati. The architectonic plan is almost the same as that of the Cathedral, the Charterhouse of Pavia and other Milanese churches in which dominates the Gothic-Lombardic style. It is the work of Guiniforte Solari. The first stone was laid on September 10th 1463. It was originally called St. Domenic's but was changed to Santa Maria delle Grazie in 1469. The interior has three naves with cross vaults, and presents, both inside and outside, the two periods and styles in which the two architects who built it worked: Solari for the three naves and Bramante for the majestic tribune. Lodovico the Moor had the Solarian apsidal removed, and in 1492 he laid the first stone of the " Tiburio ", a work favoured by his brother Cardinal Ascanio. The scarcity of proof, and the lack of documents concerning Bramante's part in the work, have always made the history of this essential part of the church uncertain. It could be the work of one of his pupils or collaborators, certainly the tribune is the hard, splendid work of a great architect. Santa Maria delle Grazie was the Moor's favourite church and he intended to make it into a great family tomb. When his young wife Beatrice d'Este died (1492) he gave Cristoforo Solari the job of carving sepulchral statues of Beatrice and himself, these were to be part of a great sepulchral cenotaph built by Giovanni della Porta. When the Sforzas fell from power the monument was dismantled and the two statues were taken to the Charterhouse of Pavia where they still lie today. In the years 1934-1937 the church was restored through the generosity of Senator E. Conti. The cloisters are very beautiful, among them, running down towards Via Caradosso, is to be found Bramante's wonderful work.

a Vinci's "Last Supper"

To the left of the church of Santa Maria delle Grazie we find the doorway to the refectory of the Domenican convent, where, on the bottom wall is painted the "Last Supper", done by Leonardo da Vinci between 1495 and 1497. Fortunately left intact after the bombing, the painting unfortunately has suffered damage of another kind — time and man. The Fine Arts Council keeps it under constant supervision, The great painting has always been in a precarious state of conservation, and even Leonardi himself, when he had finished the work, declared that the work suffered from the humidity of the ground on which the building stood. Already in 1566 Vasari said that it was crumbling. When a door was opened up in the wall, one of Christ's legs was cut, while the restorations carried out in 1726 and 1770 only helped to increase the instability of the colours. Only in in 1908 did Cavenaghi have the idea of cleaning the work and also thought of keeping the wall temperature higher than that of the room. During the last war it was miraculously saved while the refectory was destroyed. Another restoration, carried out by Mauro Pelliccioli saw to the consolidation of the entire painted surface and the salvaging of organic fragments hidden by previous restorations, which were, rather than restorations, retouchings which only brought more harm to Leonardo's work. The figures are one third bigger than life-size and show masterly particulars of execution: after having done the sketches by pen and outlining the figures in their various poses, Leonardo drew naked figures which he later dressed with colour. The painting is done in temperaforte with a technique which allowed an exquisite fineness in the passage of tones due to the perfect mixing of colours. On the opposite wall, in front of the "Last Supper", is the great "Crucifixion" painted in fresco by Donato Montorfano in 1495.

This museum, which has no egual in Italy, was founded by the engineer Guido Uccelli. It was inaugurated in 1953 with the great exhibition held for the Vth centenary of Leonardo's birth. The idea of creating a museum of this kind goes back to 1930, but it was not until 1947 that it was given the site, the suggestive Olivetano Monastery of St. Vittore. The claustral rooms — partly built on a Roman fortified enclosure which defended the mausoleum of Valentiniano II — were furnished with furniture of the period and decorated with paintings of the Lombardy school. Two rooms, chosen on an artistic basis, the monastery refectory on the ground floor and the Olivetian library, and the "Hall of Columns" on the first floor capable of seating 600 people, are often used for conferences, congresses and rallies. The museum itself, divided into section, winds through rooms especially built for it, one part is dedicated to Leonardo, this collection offers an unsurmountable collection of material which gives a complete synthethis of Leonardo's work and experiments in so many different fields, there are reproductions of his designs and plastics and mechanical models of his inventions; we can also find an experimental physics laboratory; a naval section; the museum of the history of aviation; the land transport section which has recently been enlarger by the addition of the material which was once housed in Rome's Terminal Station; there is a section dedicated to typewriters which contains the famous "Cembalo scrivano" patented by Giusepe Ravizza in 1885. There a section dedicated to clocks founded with the Parisi and Pinardi collections; the Mauro collection of silver and gold ware. The library contains 15,000 volumes on the history of science and technology. The museum is continually developing because it is often enriched by private donations and generous patrons. It is open to the public every day except Monday.

In the IVth century, between 379 and 386, St. Ambrose decided to build the church called "Basilica Martyrum" on the site of the Christian Martyrs' Cemetery, which, on the death of the saintly bishop took on his name. The paleochristian building lasted until the VIIth century. In the IXth century it was transformed into what is practically the present architectonic structures, it was during the same period that the so-called Ansperto atrium was added. The bell towers belong to different periods, the Monks' tower belongs to the IXth century, while the so-called Canonici tower belongs to the XIIth century. In 1400 the Cistercians of Chiaravalle took over from the Benedictine monks. At the end of 1400 Cardinal Ascanio Sforza the Commendatory Abbot, called Bramante to do the reconstruction work on the rectory and the monastery, but the work was left unfinished owing to the fall of the Moor. In 1630 the reconstruction work was taken up again by Francesco Maria Richini, this went on until 1797, a period in which, due to the confiscation of ecclesiastic property, the monastery was turned into a military hospital. In 1943 the church was bombed, but at the end of the war reconstruction and restoration work was immediately begun. The work went on until 1968. There is very little left of the paleochristian basilica: the "Sacello of St. Vittore in Ciel d'Oro" is very old going back to the Vth century ,its dome covered with golden tissue gives it its name. The coeval mosaics figure various saints, Ambros, Gervaso, Protaso, Materno, Naborre and Felice. The XIXth century high altar is the famous golden altar, a work of the Carolingia age done by Volvinio, the part facing the public is in gold plate whilh precious stones. The ciborium is beld up by four porphyry columns. Beneath the altar is the small chapel containing the urn with the remains of St. Ambrose, St. Gervaso and St. Protaso.

22 San Maurizio al Monastero Maggiore - The Archeological Museum - Palazzo Litta

The church of St. Maurice and the Maggiore Monastery has one side in Via Bernardino Luini and looks onto Corso Magenta. It was built by Gian Giacomo Dolcebuono between 1503 and 1509 on the ruins of a Roman building. Inside it is divided into two parts by a great wall, at the far side of which is found the claustral part from which the Benedictine nuns once listened to services. The interior contains decorations which stand out for the softness of their lines, decorations done by Bernardino Luini — one of the best artists of the late Lombardic period — whose art is revealed in the pictoric cycle of the " great wall " which divides the church, and the cycle of the martyrdom of Saint Catherine of Alessandria in the Besozzi chapel. There are other frescoes by Lombardian artists such as Antonio Campi, Bramantino, Simone Paterazzano and Luini's own sons.

The Archeological Museum is situated at the side of the church, its entrance is a monumental baroque doorway. Into one part of the Maggiore Monastery and part of the new building is incorporated the remains of the Roman walls of the Massimianea circle, and the so-called Ansperto tower which bounds the other side, this is also of Roman origin and opens onto Via Luini. The museum was opened in 1965 and is in a state of continual development. It is divided into various sections, some containing important archeological findings including the " Coppa diatreta " which came from the Trivulzian collection.

The Litta building stands in front of Via Nirone. It is a vast building, begun for Bartolomeo Arese, built mostly in the XVIIth century and completed in 1762 by the architect Bartolomeo Bolli. It has, in succession, taken on the family names of Litta-Visconti-Arese. Enriched by Pompeo Litta, it has a fine staircase designed by Giuseppe Merlo.

23 The Ambrosian Library and Its Art Gallery

Founded by Cardinal Federico Borromeo in 1609 and built by Fabio Mangone and Francesco Maria Richini, the Ambrosian Library is one of the most remarkable demonstrations of the great Federico's genius, of his love for humanistic culture and magnificence, things to which he passionately and shrewdly devoted himself. The building, which, overlooks Piazza Pio IX, was built around 1832 on the site of the demolished church of St. Maria della Rosa. The " Ambrosian " may be loosely divided into two parts: the art gallery and the library which preserves treasures of elevated culture, among which codexes, illuminated manuscripts, incunabulas and books on many varied subjects. Among these treasures can be seen Leonardo's famous " Codice Atlantico ", which after various misadventures, fell into the hands of the Marquis Arconati, who, in 1630, donated it to the " Ambrosian ". The institute has had a difficult existence, it suffered French plundering and heavy bomb damage during the air raids of 1943. The " Ambrosian " was reconstructed, on the wish of the art gallery has been rearranged, and contains, in its bright halls, masterpieces in general, but above all those of Lombardic painters. It is sufficient to remember that Leonardo's " Portrait of a Musician " is present together with works of his school, among which the portrait, presumed to be that of Beatrice d'Este, by De Predis, the " Holy Family " by Luini, and other works by Lombardic artists. Painters from the Vth. to the VIIIth. centuries are abundantly present. Sculpture is represented with the dismantled parts of the tomb of Gastone di Foix by Bambaia, whose lying statue is found in the Ancient Art Museum in the Sforzesco Castle. Raffaello's famous ' cartone ' of the " Athens School " is arranged under thick glass plate in a room especially prepared for it.

Recent studies have ascertained that the architect who built this Renaissance church of St. Maria presso St. Satiro, was in fact, D. Bramante, who built it between 1478 and 1483. It owes its architectonic unity to the brief period in which it was built. The façade, commissioned by Amadeo, however, remained just as it was planned, with only the marble base, until 1871, when the present day façade was built by the architect Giuseppe Vandoni. It was impossible to build the apse on the axis of the cross, behind the high altar, because it would have interfered with Via Falcone, so Bramante created his famous perspective, consisting of rilievi, brickwork mouldings, which were then gilded and painted, thus creating that wonderful optical illusion of a series of arches. In 1483 Bramante added the octagonal baptistery, taking his inspiration from medieval Lombardic work. Later destined to become a sacristy, it has now been restored to its original use. It is covered with brickwork decoration, the work of Agostino de Fondutis who came from Crema, and done on Bramante's designs. The so-called " Chapel of the Deposition " (a name derived from a plastic group of expressive humanity, consisting of 14 statues in painted terracotta) was originally a simple aedicule belonging to the Carolingian age, built by Ansperto de Biassono in the year 870 in his own garden. The 1938 restoration attempted to give the interior its original appearance, that is, when the square was flanked by niches which were demolished during modifications done in the Renaissance period. The cupola is supported by four monolithic columns with Corinthian capitals. Externally the chapel was closed by Bramante's Renaissance restorations. Looking towards Via Speronari, the ancient Ansperto period bell tower, is the only one in Milan which still has its ancient, IXth. century, Romanesque-Lombardic forms.

25 St. Alexander's Church - The Arcimbolde Schools - The Trivulzio Building

The first stone in the building of St. Alexander's Church was laid on March 30th. 1608 by Cardinal Federigo Borromeo. It is a majestic building in the form of a Greek cross with a central cupola resting on a tambour. The central aisle opens into a wide transept off which opens the presbytery with its semicircular choir. The precious high altar with its rare beauty, decorated with a host of precious stones and jewels set in gilded bronze, was designed by Giovan Battista Riccardi. The church is rich in decoration, frescoes and marble, it is full of inlaid wood-work, especially noteable in the confessionals and the pulpit. The church also contains numerous works of art. The face of the church is built in two parts, the lower is the work of Binago, while the upper, added in the XVIIIth. century, is in a baroquette style.

To the left of the church can be seen the building which housed the Arcimbolde Schools, a two storey building with beautiful central doors built in 1700. Inside there is a square courtyard with porticos along two sides. The upper floor is in brick with decorative panels, cornices, fasciae and other decorations, mostly around the windows. It was the seat of the Cesare Beccaria Grammar School, which has now moved, but was originally designed as a Barnabite convent school and the Arcimbolde Schools founded by Giambattista Arcimboldi, prelate of this well known Milanese family.

In front of the church can be seen the Trivulzio Building, this is a three storey building with rich cornices and a fine doorway holding up a wide balcony onto which opens the great french window above which can be seen the Trivulzio family's coat-of-arms. The palace was built by the Marquis Giorgio Trivulzio whose son Teodoro Alessandro is responsible for the famous collection of books, pictures and objects of art.

Looking down Corso Ticinese, the antique Via Marzia ,and across Piazza Vetra, you can see the sixteen Olgiascan marble columns which majestically dominate the St. Lorenzo buildings. The church stands on a raised base of wooden blocks, reproduced here, probably due to the low damp ground. The idea that St. Lorenzo was baths during the Roman Imperial periods has long been abbandoned. The studies and excavations finished in 1938, showed thas St. Lorenzo was built as an Arian basilica with an adjacent baptistery. It would appear from St. Ambrose's writings that it was the Portian Basilica built about 350 A.C. The interior is a square hall and the cupola rises majestically above it. It is surrounded by three very ancient chapels or small basilicas; according to recent studies the one dedicated to St. Aquilino, also called the "Regina" chapel — because apparently the queen Galla Placidia wanted to be buried here — was an Arian baptistery. The main doorway, which was brought from another building, is in finely carved marble, while inside there are IVth century mosaics. The St. Ippolito chapel has four white marble columns with very fine capitals. The St. Sisto chapel was added by the Bishop Lorenzo at the end of the Vth century. The basilica of St. Lorenzo was, until the end of the VIth century, considered one of Milan's greatest monuments because of its characteristic towers which are still today, the main supporting structure. The cupola was hemispherical and richly decorated with mosaics. It had been the victim of various fires and was rebuilt in the Romanesque period; in 1573 it underwent its last collapse and was rebuilt a few years later in the way we see it today. However, the various reconstructions have not altered the primitive structure. The statue of the Emperor Constantine stands in the square to remind us, that here in Milan, in 313, he decreed the edict of free worship.

27 St. Eustorgio and the Portinari Chapel

The basilica of St. Eustorgio is an architectonical assembly of the IXth and XIIth centuries with additions made in the XIVth and XVI centuries. It was founded by Eustorgio II who buried the remains of the Three Kings, brought from the East, in it. Many legends grew up about the Three Kings, but one is certain, that Archbishop Rainaldo, following Barbarosso, took them to his city and built the famous cathedral in Cologne to keep them in. The Eustorgio basilica is one of the most important in Milan and clearly shows the various periods of its construction. It was the favourite church of the Viscontis and da Ottones and Filippo Maria enlarged it. It contains sculptures by Giovanni di Balduccio of Pisa, among which can be seen the altar-piece of the Three King's altar and the frontal of the high altar. There are two cloisters beside the church built in 1300 for the Domenican monks. It underwent rebuilding in 1600 which is not entirely lacking in elegance. The convent was used as the headquarters for the court of the Lombardian Inquisition. When the order was abolished in 1798 the convent became a miliary barracks and put to other uses. The city council is trying to free it of the old buildings, and together with other buildings, make it into an art gallery. From Piazza St. Eustorgio the overall effect of the buildings is one of architectual harmony dominated by the bell tower which, after the one in St. Gottardo in Palazzo, is the most elegant in Milan. Beyond the back part of the choir of the basilica is found the Portinari chapel, called the chapel of St. Peter the Martyr because it contains the tomb in which the saint's body is buried. The harmonious Gothic sculptures are the work of Balduccio of Pisa and his assistants. The building was erected by Pigello Portinari and is a mixure of Tuscan and Lombardian architecture. Perhaps Amadeo helped in its construction too, the frescoes on the walls are the work of Foppa.

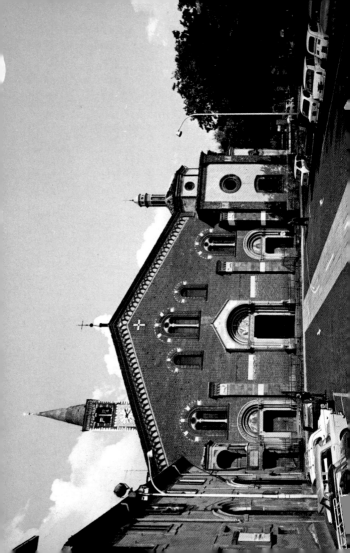

28 The Sanctuary of St. Maria and the church of St. Celso

The sanctuary is built beside the none less famous church of St. Celso in Corso Italia. Legend has it that there was once a field there called "the three Moors", in which — according to one of Paolino's chronicles — the bodies of the two martyrs Nazaro and Celso were found. While Nazaro's body was taken to the basilica of the Apostles, the present-day St. Nazaro, Celso's body was left in the field, and here was erected the church which bears his name. The ancient Lombard — Romanesque building we see today is not the one begun by bishop Landolfo II of Carcano in 992; its structure is XIth century or even XIIth. The front was moved back when four arches were demolished and rebuilt where it stands today but preserving the original doorway with its beautiful sculptured architrave and carved pannelled wooden doors, built in 1454. The solid bell tower is one of the most beautiful and best preserved in Milan. The sanctuary of St. Mary of the Miracles was built next to a chapel under Filippo Maria Visconti's orders in 1430 to contain a small wall on which was painted a Madonna which was believed to work miracles. The first projects for the sanctuary (1493) were drawn un by Dolcebuona but others supervised the work. The beautiful front was designed by Galeazzo Alessi; when he died in 1572 the work was continued, with various modifications, by Marino Bassi. The porticos in front are the work of Cesare Cesariano. Inside there are decorations, frescoes, painting and sculptures done by Lombardian artists of the fifteenth, sixteenth and seventeenth centuries. The floor is a mosaic of multicoloured stone and marble. The presbytery and high altar offer an appearance of uncomparable beauty with their precious stones giving an extraordinary effect. The sanctuary cotains a treasure of unestimative value among which the famous, so-called Chiaravalle cross in gold and crystal.

29 St. Nazaro In Brolo's
(Ancient Basilica Degli Apostoli)

St. Nazaro's is a palaeochristian basilica built by St. Ambrogio in 382. Firstly it was called Basilica Degli Apostoli; when St. Ambrogio took there St. Nazaro's corpse, found at the "Campo The Mori" together with Martyr Celso's one, it was called St. Nazaro Al Corpo's Basilica. Before the church there was a roman christian graveyard; an arcade linked the basilica to Corso Di Porta Romana which was called Via Porticata because of the house-porches all along the street. The church, damaged by a fire and rebuilt in 1075, was subjected to various tamperings; recently its architectural structure has been brought back to its Lombard Romanesque shapes. Near St. Nazaro's, towards Via Osti, there is St. Caterina's small church or chapel, a beautiful Renaissance building with a "tiburio" inspired by Bramante (1500). A wall is covered by a large fresco painted by Lanino, "St. Caterina's Martyrdom".

The basilica front does not exist any longer because in 1512 the Trivulzio funerary chapel was built before it, under the form of a vestibule. The octagonal interior is typical of the first Lombard baptisteries. It was built to become Trivulzios' mausoleum, and to contain, together with their tombs, also the equestrian monument representing Gian Giacomo Trivulzio, Marshal of France, ordered to Leonardo. While outside it was not finished, inside the building offers a view of exceptionally hardy and, at the same time, severe architectural lines. It was designed by Bartolomeo Suardi, called "Bramantino".

This buildings is better known as the "Ca' Granda", which means the home which accepts everybody, the original idea was a decision taken by Archibishop Enrico Rampini, who — during the period of the "Golden Ambrosian Republic" — wanted to unite all the various hospitals spread around the city. It was officially founded by Francesco Sforza moved by his wife Bianca Maria Visconti. The Florentine architect Antonio Averulino, known as Filarete, was called upon for the construction, and be designed the great building and began the work. Guiniforte Solari, a milanese, succeded him in 1465; while Ludovico the Moor was in power Antonio Amadeo was engaged and he intergrated and perfected the work on the same lines as those of Filarete. He built the great doorway an the ground floor and the first floor portico in the great courtyard. Some of the exquisite marble medallions are his work too. The front the hospital looks over Via Festa del Perdono and stretches for 260 meters, offering its exceptionally artistic greatness and nobility. The part looking towards St. Nazaro goes from Largo Richini to Via F. Sforza, this is the oldest part and was built on Filarete's original designs. It is enriched by a portico on the first floor and by arched mullion windows, work of Solari, on the second. The median part, built with the Carcano legacy shows structures done by Richini, Mangone and others who all decided to work on the fifteenth century model with Gothic windows and brick medaillons, but with an obvious baroque touch. But at the end of the seventeenth century, with the Macchio legacy, the last part, looking towards Via Laghetto, was begun, construction went on through the eighteen hundreds. With the building of the new hospital at Niguarda (1938), the "Ca' Granda" was left vacant, later to become the seat of the State University, the Chancellorate, and the humanistic faculties of the university.

St. Maria Della Passione's Church rises between
Via Conservatorio and Via V. Bellini. It was built
by oder of Domenico Birago, Prothonotary Apos-
tolical, appointed by Sisto IV as Church Collector
in Milan and entitled Archibishop of Mitilene. The
church was assigned to the Lateran Canons and it
was almost finished in 1485. The octagonal two-
ranges dome and the apse were designed by Cristoforo Solari called "Humpback". The baroque
front, built later on, seems to be mutilated because
of its limited height. Since 1808 the annexe convent
has been the seat of the Academy of Music "G.
Verdi". The church interior with three aisles was
reconstructed several times. It contains various
Lombard Renaissance pictures as, for instance:
"The Deposition from the Cross" by Bernardino
Luini, "The Redeemer" by Ambrogio Da Fossano,
"The Supper" by Gaudenzio Ferrari, "The Calvary"
by Don Pietro Bocchi Da Bagnara, "St. Francesco
D'Assisi" by Camillo Procaccini, "St. Carlo Borro-
meo's fast" by Daniele Crespi. The sacristy dome
was adorned and frescoed by Bergognone. Daniela
Birago's sepulchral monument was built by Andrea
Fusina in 1495.

32 St. Maria Alla Fontana

In the district, also called "The island", outside
Porta Comasina, at the end of Via Borsieri there
is St. Maria alla Fontana's Sacellum (Via Thaon
Di Revel) which was started in 1507 after a mir-
aculous recovery.
The building is formed by two churches built one
upon the other, the more valuable of which is
the lower one. A staircase with a barrel vault leads
to a crypt flanked by two cloisters with arcades
that go all round the Oratory, which has a square
plan, with an umbrella-vault and mullioned doors.
The building, with its Renaissance decorations
gives an impression of limpidity and space. Its
construction was attributed to Leonardo but more
up-to-date critics ascribe it to some of his disciples.
Somebody has also thought of Bramante, Bramantino and Dolcebuono. Recently the sacellum has
been restored giving it back its original meaning
of sanctuary and bringing into use again the foun-
tain springs which gave the name to the sanctuary.
In any case, St. Maria Alla Fontana's sanctuary is
one of the monuments built during the Sforza
period or soon after it, in which Leonardo inter-
vened if not always practically, at least giving
his advices.
The upper church has not a particular artistic
value, even being rather important: Guido Bom-
barda seems to be its author but many other
names have been mentioned.

33 The Charterhouse of Garegnano

It was founded in 1359 by Giovanni Visconti Archbishop of Milan and his brother Luchino in the village of Garegnano, which had already become part of the city of Milan. Coming into Milan from the motorway to the lakes, you can see monumental assembly of the charterhouse from the apsis side with its late sixteenth century refacings, with brick decorations belonging to the previous building. It offers a harmonious view of proportioned equilibrium. It can be reached from Viale Certosa by turning into Via Garegnano and reaching Via Pareto which, from Piazzale del Cimitero Maggiore, leads to the entrance, where a doorway opens onto a vestibule beyond which opens the poligonal courtyard, with the church as a background. The simple-lined, well balanced façade is the work of the able hands of Galeazzo Alessi, called in to reface it between 1560 and 1570. It also seems that Seregni, Alessi's contemporary, is not to be completely excluded from its execution as their work is very similar and one is often mistaken for the other. Besides the architectonic assembly, the main attractions are the frescoes which Daniele Crespi painted between 1628 and 1629, these illustrate the life of St. Brunone, founder of the order of Carthusian monks. The most expressive painting is the one which illustrates the funeral of the Parisian doctor Raimondo Diocrés, and it is said that Lord Byron stood in ecstasy in front of it for hours on end. Other than Crespi's celebrated frescoes there are painting by Peterzano, Bellotti, Genovesino and Salmeggia. Francesco Petrach stopped in the Linterno Villa in 1357, he went there to inhale the perfume of the "closed garden of Garegnano" where one of his brothers, Gerardo, was a monk. Many famous people have stayed at the charterhouse, among them St. Carlo Borromeo and his cousin Federico; Philip IV, king of Spain, and his brother the Archbishop of Toledo.

34 The Abbey of Chiaravalle Milanese

This was founded in 1135 by St. Bernanrd of Clair-
vaux, which in Italian was translated as Chiaravalle (Clearvalley). The Cistercian monks, an order
founded by the Abbot Roberto in Borgogna in
1980, went to live there. When Bernard of Chiara-
vallewas called to Milan at the beginning of the
XII century to settle a quarrel between the Pope
and the Emperor, he satisfied the wish of the Milanese people by founding the Abbey, which became
famous by bringing, for the first time, Cistercian
puritanism, to us. The first stone was laid on
January 22nd. 1135 and the building was begun. The
present day church, however, is not the original
one, but the one built during the next century and
altered by later restorations. The architecture, is
a Gothic-Burgundia style mixed with Lombardie
elements; the fine tower, rising above the tiburium, is characteristic, and its structure, with the
wide use of brick, reminds us of St. Gottardo in
Corte, so much so as to make us think that the
author is the same, Francesco Pecorari di Cremona.
The interior has three naves, divided by eight pillars, once fasciaed, covered with cilindrical mason-
ry, architecture which in 1600 was once more disfigured. The tiburium contains fourteenth century
frescoes of the Giotto school. At the top of the
staircase which linked the church to the dormitory,
there is a fresco painting portraving the Virgin
and Child by Bernardino Luini (1512). The two tran-
scepts, the counter façade and the two great frescoes above the choir are the seventeenth century
work of the two brothers Mauro and Giambattista
delle Rovere called the "Fiammenghini". The choir
stalls, some of the most famous in Italy, are the
masterpiece of the Milanese engraver Carlo Gara-
vaglia (1645) who took 53 years to finish them;
on them are portrayed the life, miracles and death
of St. Bernard. From the transcept, a small door
on the left, opens onto the cemetery which stands

behind the church; on one side, against the outer wall, are found the sepuchral chapels with the noble coats-of-arms of the Della Torre, Archinti and other noble Milanese families. In one of these was buried the famous Guglielmina Boema, this woman was considered a saint when she died, in 1282, but was later considered a heretic, and then her mortal remains were removed, burned and the ashes dispersed. With the suspension of the monastical order (1798) the Abbey's property was confiscated and the building mutilated, later it was destined to rural use, a thing which, of course, hastened its decadence. Only during this century has any attention been paid to it, and when in 1952, the first Cistercian monks returned to Chiaravalle, restoration work was begun. Of the small cloisters only the ruins against the side of the church remained, and a part of the destroyed chapter room. Their certain destruction was spared, and with materials recovered on the site — pillars, arches and column heads, reconstruction work was begun on the two missing wings, while the fourth, into which opens the great refectory, has been built ex-novo, but the addition can be seen from the three great brick arches.

35 The Viboldone Abbey

From the centre of Milan, following Corso di Porta Romana, Corso Lodi and the Via Emilia. you come to the village of St. Giuliano, and having passed through the village, taking the first turn to the right, onto the local road, you reach the minute hamlet built arond the abbey itself, this is one of the most famous Lombardic monuments. The ancient Abbey of Viboldone was founded in the XIIth. century by the Umiliati monks, e religious-lay order whose origin goes back to those Milanese who were deported to Germany as hostages, on returning home, after having paid their ransome, congregated under the name of the "Umiliated", fixing their home in the mother-house of Brera. They fonuded this abbey in 1176, but its construction was carried on during the next century and was completed in 1348. The church, the surviving building, is a Romanesque construction with Gothic elements. The façade is solemn, but the interiore is silent and mystic. The fourteenth century frescoes are of great value, these decorate the walls and the vaults of the two main bays. They were cleaned about thirty years ago, and at that time it was decided that they were painted in 1349, a date which can be read under the fresco done on the tiburium, this represents the Madonna on a throne, but the author remains unknown. The major critics have mentioned the name of Giovanni da Milano, and quite rightly, that of Giusto de' Menabuoi. Due to the plague that raged in Florence in 1348, a group of painters, in order to escape the plague, came to Lombardy and found hospitality in the Abbey at Viboldone. It was on this occasion, that the Umiliati, wanting to decorate their church, asked the painters to adorn it. Then the group spread out all over Lombardy, and traces of their work can be found in the oratories of Solaro, Mocchirolo, Lentate and at Albizzate.

The Abbey of Mirasole stands in the lowlands of Milan among green marshy meadows of rushy grass. It is reached by following the Vigentine provincial road to Pavia; after going through the villages of Noverasco and Quintosole a yellow finger post on the right, indicates the road leading to the Abbey. The Umiliati of Brera came here long ago, in 1200, and erected one of the most famous "grangia" (farm and monastery), that of Mirasole. The building does not live up to its fascinating sunny name, as, in fact, it is a very foggy place, especially during the cold seasons. The name owes its origin simply to the orientation of the church, whose façade, at midday, faces the sun, a characteristic of all Umiliati churches. The entrance, which opens onto a courtyard, consists of a solid tower, once fortified by a draw bridge crossing the moat which surrounded the "grangia", this was a necessary construction for all isolated buildings in the country, at that time exposed to bands of robbers who roamed the countryside, and even against the plundering of passing soldiers. In spite of the rough treatment of the centuries, Mirasole has survived until today, with the disposition of the buildings almost entirely as they originally were. The building is a proof of the sociale and economic phenomena which followed, in a certain sense, the present day industrialization of agriculture. The history of Mirasole is tightly bound to the history of the Umiliati. According to Giulini, in 1257 there were seven monks, and in 1272 the provost of Badia was elected General of the Order. The development of the building took place in different periods. The church dates back to 1300 while the cloisters belong to 1400, above the cloisters, on two sides a loggia was added. In 1571 the order was suspended and the vast farm was entrusted to Monsignor Marco Lanetta on behalf of Cardinal Altemps. Later it passed, together with all the ground, to the Swiss College and remained theirs until 1787, the year in which Napoleon I gave the ground and buildings to the Maggiore Hospital in Milan as a sign of gratitude for the care taken of his men by the hospital itself. After that the "grangia" was rented out to tenant farmers, and it was then that its abandon set in, so much so, that one side of the cloisters was transformed into the manager's living quarters. In 1939 restoration of the church was carried out, but this was a kind of rescue in extremis. In 1960 definite restoration work was begun, and in 1964 the church was reopened to worship. The fresco paintings of the apse, the high altar and the sixteenth century chapel came back to life. Now, the foundations of the bell tower above the church have been reinforced, and work is still being carried out to repair the entire architectural assembly.

The Charterhouse of Pavia is reached by following the State road No. 35 for Genoa, for about 25 kilometers (Torre del Mangano), then taking the road through the village, along the tree-lined avenue which leads to the vast square in front of the building. The first stone of the charterhouse was laid by Gian Galeazzo Visconti on August 27th. 1396 on the wish of his second wite Catherina Visconti, daughter of Barnabò. It was built with the name of St. Maria delle Grazie and was intended to be the mausoleum of the Visconti family. The first architect was Bernardo da Conigo but Giacomo da Como and Cristoforo da Conigo also took part in the work, and even perhaps, Giovannino de' Grassi and Marco da Carona who were already working on the cathedral in Milan. In 1420 Giovanni Solari appreared on the site and in 1453 his son Guiniforte Solaris seems to have taken part. The presence of the Pavian . A. Amadeo is determinative, being one of the sculptors, engineers and architects of the building. Beside him worked Cristoforo and Antonio Mantegazza, Milanese goldsmiths and sculptors whose work was done in the years between 1464 and 1495. The most suggestive element of the Charterhouse is the magnificent façade of extraordinary beauty. The interior has three naves with a Gothic framework and faciaded pillars. The transcept is divided by a rich iron and bronze rail, beyond which stands the choir and high altar. The oldest sculpture in the triptych carved from a hippopotamus tooth, this is to be found in the old vestry, and is the work of the Florentine Baldassare degli Embriachi done between 1400 and 1409. In the left transcept is the tomb stone, with the lying statues of Beatrice d'Este and Lodovico the Moor. The assembly of the coenoby consists of, other than the church, the Abbot's palace, the small cloisters and the great cloisters with the monks' cells.

ACADEMIES

Accademia arti applicate - c. Venezia, 8 - Tel. 705071
Accademia Cimabue d'arte cultura musica - v. S. Calimero, 4 - Tel. 542477
Accademia Crosignani - v. Plinio, 16 - Tel. 265140
Accad. del Mediterraneo - v. Lamarmora, 40 - Tel. 581042
Accademia di Attività Artistiche « Ateneo Artistico 3 A » - Scuola Femminile - v. Mazzini, 10 - Tel. 871771
Accad. di Belle Arti di Brera - Presidente - v. Brera, 28 - Tel. 871379 - Liceo Artistico - v. Barabino, 4 - Tel. 533287 - Liceo Artistico - p. XXV Aprile, 8 - Tel. 638676 - Scuola di Architett. - v. Brera, 28 - Tel. 807986 - Liceo Artistico - v. Bugatti, 2 - Tel. 8488733 - Scuola di Pittura - v. Brera, 28 - Tel. 804446 - Scuola di Scenografia - v. Brera, 28 - Tel. 804388 - Cattedra Decorazione e Affresco - v. Brera, 28 - Tel. 867358
Accademia Italiana della Cucina - v. Agnello, 2 - Tel. 860360

AIRPORTS

Aeroporto della Malpensa - Gallarate - Tel. 868041
S.E.A., Aeroporto della Malpensa - Tel. 868028
S.E.A. - vl. E. Forlanini (Aeroporto Forlanini) - Tel. 717042

TRAVELLING AGENCIES

Gran Turismo - v. Monte Napoleone, 5 - Tel. 798214
Agenzia Viaggi Chiariva - v. Dante, 8 - Tel. 867431 - Autostaz. Foro Buonaparte, 8 - Tel. 803016
AIOC - l.go Domodossola, 1 - Tel. 315401
Air Agency Gondrand - p. Fidia, 1 - Tel. 6088
Airtour Italia - p. Velasca, 5 - Tel. 8690708
Aliviaggi p. Po 6 - Tel. 4695136
American Express Company - v. Pisani, 19 - Tel. 669721
A.R.S. - Agenzia Ricezione Stranieri - v. Durini, 17 - Telefono 790808
A.T.I. - c. Lodi, 2 - Tel. 559177
A.T.I.G. - v. Festa del Perdono, 10 - Tel. 861700
Atlantic Office - v. Albricci 8 - Tel. 807361
Atlas - c. Buenos Aires, 6- Tel. 225101
Atlas - v. Orefici, 26 - Tel. 899970
Atlas Viaggi - v. Omenoni, 2 - Tel. 704455
Autostradale - p. Castello, 1 - Tel. 867631
Autostradale - v. Mercanti, 21 - Tel. 872621
Autoturistica - p. della Repubblica, 12 - Tel. 632432

A.V.E.V. - v. Farini, 91 - Tel. 683830
A.V.E.V. - vl. Porta Vercellina — - Tel. 483500
Avior Viaggi - v. Pola, 4 - Tel. 600407
Away Ambrosiana - v. Turati, 7 - Tel. 654331
Bonomi & Pagani - v. Paolo da Cannobio, 2 - Tel. 899713
Camel - vl. Abruzzi, 12 - Tel. 2041950
Centropa - v. Turati, 8 - Tel. 654261
Centro Turistico della Tunisia - v. Albricci, 10 - **Tel.** 871126
Certosa - p. Firenze, 12/14 - Tel. 323841
Chiari e Sommariva - v. Dante, 8 - Tel. 867431
Cipriani - Gall. Doria, 56 - Tel. 266591
C.I.A.T. - Gall. Carrozze Staz. Centrale - Tel. 220224 - **Gall.**
   Vitt. Emanuele - **Tel.** 871470
C.I.S.I.T. - p. Missori, 2 - Tel. 892537
C.I.T. - Gall. Vitt. Eman. - Tel. 866661
C.L.I. - c. Vitt. Emanuele, 13 - Tel. 793882
Cobianchi - p. del Duomo - Tel. 807064
Continental Viaggi - v. Corridoni, 1 - Tel. 700207
Corvetto - vl. Martini, 9 - Tel. 5392911
Dan Viaggi - s.r.l. - v. S. Paolo, 13 - Tel. 803417
Delta Viaggi - vl. Beatrice d'Este, 48 - Tel. 544238
Diners Fugazy Intern. - p. S. Maria Beltrade, 1 - Tel.
   896312
Duomo - Viaggi e Turismo - v. S. Antonio, 5 - Tel. 893488
Ente Naz. Austriaco Turismo - v. Dogana, 2 - Tel. 803532
Ente Provinciale per il Turismo - St. Centrale - Tel. 206030
Ente Provinciale per il Turismo - v. Marconi, 1 - Tel.
   870016 - 870416 - 897015
Ermes Viaggi - c. Europa, 22 - Tel. 782200
Euramerica - c. Buenos Aires, 66 - Tel. 228703
Europe at Cost Ltd. - v. Olmetto, 5 - Tel. 800323
Fabello - v. Anfossi, 36 - Tel. 541735
Farè N. - v. Mazzini, 20 - Tel. 800777
Farotto Viaggi - v. Gallarate, 131 - Tel. 3081576
Ferrovie Britanniche - v. Pirelli, 11 - Tel. 667964
Ferti Viaggi - v. Turati, 30 - Tel. 653941
Generaltours - v. S. Maria Segreta, 9 - Tel. 802074
Global of London - v. Camperio, 9 - Tel. 890968
Gran Turismo - v. Monte Napoleone, 5 - Tel. 798214
Hotur - v. Paolo da Cannobio, 11 - Tel. 878643
I grandi viaggi - p. Diaz, 2 - Tel. 896604
Intermas - p. Velasca, 6 - Tel. 867883
Italnord Lloyd - v. V. Pisani, 7 - Tel. 654251

Italo Orientale Viaggi e Tur. - v. Morone, 8 - Tel. 790296
Italturismo - p. Duca d'Aosta - Tel. 266039
Italturist - v. Baracchini, 10 - Tel. 8690641
Ivet - v. S. Sofia, 9 - Tel. 545551
Kuoni Viaggi - v. Paolo da Cannobio, 10 - Tel. 8690736
Mediterranean Holidays - p. Missori, 2 - Tel. 873421
Milan Express - v. Puccini, 1 - Tel. 897194
Milan Personal Services - c. Italia, 11 - Tel. 892749
Mondialtur - c. Venezia, 43 - Tel. 706350
Mondorama - v. Fontana, 22 - Tel. 780104
Moteltour (S. Donato Milanese) - v. Alfonsine, 6 - Tel.
    512232
O.I.E.C. Studi e Vacanze all'Estero - v. Broletto, 44 -
    Tel. 866310
Oltremare - v. Baracchini, 11 - Tel. 896358
Oriental Viaggi - v. Washington, 106 - Tel. 470327
Pierbusseti - v. Pisani, 26 - Tel. 653638
Rimoldi Autolinee - p. de Angeli, 12 - Tel. 468441
Rinaldi Viaggi e Turismo srl - c. Venezia, 6 - Tel. 702293
Riviera Express - p. Cadorna, 10 - Tel. 861456
Rose Tours - v. Vitruvio, 43 - Tel. 202527
Sea Viaggi - p. Duca d'Aosta, 7/a - Tel. 654044
SGEA - p. Cadorna, 2 - Tel. 896031
Sicilea - c. Vittorio Emanuele II, 37/3 - Tel. 708072
S.I.O. - v. Morone, 8 - Tel. 791568
S.I.T.A.V. - v. S. Pietro all'Orto, 9 - Tel. 780027
S.T.E.S. - v. Cavallotti, 13 - Tel. 792417
Tecnitour srl - p. Amendola, 3 - Tel. 435414
Tesi - v. Manzoni, 21 - Tel. 879512
Tours Jet p. Giordano, 4 - Tel. 702696
Transalpino - v. Locatelli, 5 - Tel. 650898
Transitalia Viaggi - v. Pattari, 2 - Tel. 865398
Travelclub - vl. Pasubio, 3 - Tel. 661666
Trisair - v. Copernico, 30/A - Tel. 6881340
Turisanda - v. Pellico, 8 - Tel. 862553
Turistica Italiana A.T.I. - c. Genova, 3 - Tel. 851341
Uff. Naz. Spagnolo Turismo - v. Del Don, 5 - Tel. 897476
Uff. Viaggi e Turismo Ambrosiani (diurno Venezia) - p.
    Oberdan - Tel. 203602
Uff. Viaggi e Turismo Ferrovie Nord Milano - pl. Cador-
    na, 14 - Tel. 896332
Union Viaggi e Crociere - v. Vittorio Emanuele, 30 - Tel.
    702422

UTRAS Viaggi e Turismo - v. Manzoni, 38 - Tel. 782441
U.V.E.T. - vl. Ferdinando di Savoia, 2 - Tel. 652589
Vacanze - p. Diaz, 1 Tel. 878491
Vacanze Studio all'Estero - v. Turati, 3 - Tel. 635113
Viaggi « Doria » - p. Duca D'Aosta - Tel. 265398
Viaggi e Turismo 5 Giornate - p. 5 Giornate - Tel. 795177
Viaggi Fiorentino - v. Durini, 27 - Tel. 706258
Viaggi Hotelplan Italia - c. Italia, 1 - Tel. 806223
Viaggi Marco - p. Luigi di Savoia, 2 - Tel. 203720
Viaggi « Meravigli » - v. Meravigli, 14 - Tel. 860773
Viaggi Ticinese - p. S. Eustorgio, 4 - Tel. 830233
Viaggi Turismo Cambio « Rinaldi » - p. Duomo, 6 - Tel.
897048
Viaggi Turismo Cobianchi - p. Duomo ang. Pellico - **Tel.**
807064
Viaggi Visitando il mondo - v. Montenero, 6 - Tel. 581075
Viaggi Volta - v. Volta, 10 - Tel. 637985
Wagon-Lits Cook - v. Manzoni, 10 - Tel. 877641
Yogotours - v. Agnello, 18 - Tel. 877741

HOTELS
Luxury Cathegory
Cavalieri (dei) - p.za Missori 1 - Tel. 8857
Continentale Grand Hotel - via Manzoni, 7 - Tel. 807641
Excelsior Gallia - p.za Duca d'Aosta, 9 - **Tel. 6277**
Grand Hotel Duomo - via S. Raffaele, 1 - Tel. 8833
Grand Hotel Et de Milan - via Manzoni, 29 - Tel. 870757
Hilton Hotel - v. Galvani, 12 - Tel. 6983
Hotel Anderson - p. Luigi di Savoia, 20 - Tel. 2043741
Palace Hotel - p. della Repubblica, 20 - Tel. 6336
Principe & Savoia - p. della Repubblica, 17 - Tel. 6230

1st Cathegory
Aerhotel Fiera - v.le Boezio, 20 - Tel. 3105
Amedei - via Amedei, 2 - Tel. 897065
Anderson - p. Luigi di Savoia, 20
Ascot - v. Lentasio, 3/5 - Tel. 862946
Auriga Hotel - via Pirelli, 7 - Tel. 632851
Carlton Senato - via Senato, 5 - Tel. 781780
Cavour - via Fatebenefratelli, 23 - Tel. 650983
Diana Majestic - v.le Piave, 42 - Tel. 270487
Florida - via Lepetit, 33 - Tel. 266910
Francia Europa - c.so Vitt. Emanuele II, 9 - Tel. 708301
Hotel de la Ville - via Hoepli, 6 - Tel. 867651

Jolly Hotel President - l.go Augusto, 10 - Tel. 794459
Lloyd - c. Romana, 48 - Tel. 867971
Manin - via Manin, 7 - Tel. 667251
Marino alla Scala - p.za della Scala, 5 - Tel. 867803
Michelangelo - v. Scarlatti, 33 - Tel. 2055
Plaza - Grand Hotel - p. Diaz, 3 - Tel. 898752
Rosa - v. Pattari, 5 - Tel. 896443
Royal Hotel - v. Cardano, 1 - Tel. 653641
Select - via Baracchini, 12 - Tel. 8843
Splendido - v. Doria, 4 - Tel. 2041841
Touring e Gran Turismo - v. Tarchetti, 2 - Tel. 665653
Windsor - v. G. Galilei, 2 - Tel. 637151

2nd Cathegory

Adam - via Palmanova, 153 - Tel. 2564750
Adriatico - v. Conca del Naviglio, 20 - Tel. 8474141
Agape - via Flumendosa, 35 - Tel. 2566691
Alexander - via Napo Torriani, 9 - Tel. 654006
Ambasciatori - gall. del Corso, 3 - Tel. 701472
Ambrosiano Hotel - via S. Sofia, 9 - Tel. 580445
American Hotel - via Finocchiaro Aprile, 2 - Tel. 666441
Andreola - via Scarlatti, 24 - Tel. 220641
Aosta - p.za Duca d'Aosta, 14 - Tel. 266481
Ariosto Hotel - via Ariosto, 22 - Tel. 490995
Ariston - lg. Carrobbio, 2 - Tel. 897286
Astoria Hotel - v.le Murillo, 9 - Tel. 405790
Augustus - via Torriani, 29 - Tel. 665054
Baviera e Stazione - via Castaldi, 7 - Tel. 639690
Berna - via Torriani, 18 - Tel. 203819
Biscione - v. S. Maria Fulcorina, 15 - Tel. 879903
Bristol Schmid - via Scarlatti, 32 - Tel. 203751
Cairoli - via Porlezza, 4 - Tel. 877177
Canada - via Lentasio, 15 - Tel. 892527
Canova - v. Napo Torriani, 15 - Tel. 650098
Capitol Hotel - via Cimarosa, 6/8 - Tel. 430526
Centro - via Broletto, 46 - Tel. 875232
City Hotel - c.so Buenos Aires, 42/5 - Tel. 228379
Colombia - via Lepetit, 15 - Tel. 203818
Cristallo - via Scarlatti, 22 - Tel. 2042101
Crivi's - via Crivelli, 27 - Tel. 5463341
Delle Nazioni - via A. Cappellini, 18 - Tel. 654931
Del Teatro Principe - via S. Mansueto, 3 - Tel. 580511
D'Este - v.le Bligny, 23 - Tel. 5461041

Domus - **p. Gerusalemme, 6** - Tel. 3490251
Esperia & Corona - via Tenca, 21 - Tel. 632338
Fiera - **v. Spinola, 9** - **Tel. 432472**
Flora Hotel - via Torriani, 23 - Tel. 639518
Gamma - via Valvassori Peroni, 85 - Tel. 292061
Garda - via Torriani, 21 - Tel. 635169
Imperial - c.so P. Romana, 68 - Tel. 541520
King - c. Magenta, 19 - Tel. 874432
Lido - via R. Galli, 8 - Tel. 364030
Lombardia - v.le Lombardia, 74 - Tel. 2824817
Lord Hotel Internazionale - via Spadari, 11 - Tel. 803028
Madison - via Gasparotto, 8 - Tel. 6085991
Manzoni Hotel - via S. Spirito, 20 - Tel. 705697
Mayor - via Isonzo, 2 - Tel. 544091
Mec - via Tito Livio, 4 - Tel. 544040
Mediolanum Hotel - via Macchi, 1 - Tel. 225834
Mediterraneo - v. Muratori, 14 - Tel. 558151
Mennini Hotel - via Boscovich, 22 - Tel. 228951
Metrò - **c. Vercelli, 61**
Moderno - via Mazzini, 4 - Tel. 871907
Molise - v. Cadibona, 2 - Tel. 5464013
Monopole Hotel de la Gare - via Filzi, 43 - Tel. 600831
Monte Rosa - v. Monte Rosa, 90 - Tel. 4697941
Napoleon - v. Ozanam, 12 - Tel. 208280
New York - v. Pirelli, 5 - Tel. 650551
Pedrotti - **p.le Lotto, 14** - **Tel. 324229**
Piemonte - v. R. Settimo, 1 - Tel. 439939
Plinius Hotel - v. Plinio, 2 - Tel. 203889
Regina Metropole - v. S. Margherita, 16 - Tel. 803958
Rio - v. Mazzini, 8 - Tel. 874114
Ritter - c. G. Garibaldi, 68 - Tel. 650039
Rubens - via Rubens, 21 - Tel. 405051
S. Carlo - v. Torriani, 28 - Tel. 203022
San Guido - v. Farini, 1/A - Tel. 662261
Sant'Ambroeus - vl. Papiniano, 14 - Tel. 4697451
Scala Nord - v. Ferruccio, 10/a - Tel. 316041
Sempione - via Finocchiaro Aprile, 11 - Tel. 665285
Settebello Hotel - v. Catalani, 69 - Tel. 2893828
St. George - v. Tunisia, 9 - Tel. 206375
Star - v. Bossi, 5 - Tel. 871703
Teco - v. Spallanzani, 27 - Tel. 270021
Terminus - vl. Vittorio Veneto, 32 - Tel. 639742
Vittoria di **Marchesi** G. - v. Calvi, 32 - Tel. 780126

Wagner - via Buonarroti, 13 - Tel. 4696051
Zefiro - via Gallina, 12 - Tel. 7384253
Zurigo - c. Italia, 11/a - Tel. 808909

3rd Cathegory

Accursio - v.le Certosa, 88 - Tel. 390270
Adler - via Ricordi, 10 - Tel. 221441
Alba - v.le Certosa, 68 - Tel. 395061
Apollo - **v. Ripamonti, 102 - Tel. 5396987**
Archimede - via Archimede, 81 - Tel. 718185
Arena - v. Giulianova, 2 - Tel. 802015
Argentina Poste Suisse - via Filzi, 3 - Tel. 665503
Bassano - via Bassano del Grappa, 28 - Tel. 287607
Berlino Hotel - via Plana, 33 - Tel. 367732
Bernina - via Torriani, 27 - Tel. 652185
Bolzano - via Boscovich, 21 - Tel. 635094
Boston - via Lepetit, 7 - Tel. 206317
Bruxelles - p. Castello, 13 - Tel. 861404
Buenos Aires - c.so Buenos Aires, 26 - Tel. 225358
Ca' Granda - v. Porpora, 87 - Tel. 2850295
Campionaria - v.le Berengario, 3 - **Tel. 462363**
Candidezza - via Unione, 8 - Tel. 806668
Casella - v.le Certosa, 106 - Tel. 395938
Castelletto - **via Archimede, 79 - Tel. 7383021**
Catalani e Madrid - via Catalani, 71 - Tel. 286361
Certosa - c. S. Gottardo, 7 - Tel. 851105
Cervo - p.le pr. Clotilde, 10 - Tel. 639724
Cincinnato - via S. Giovanni alla Paglia, 9 - Tel. 666929
Città Studi - via Saldini, 24 - Tel. 744602
Corallo Hotel - via Cesena, 20 - Tel. 314074
Corvetto Hotel - p.le Corvetto, 5 - Tel. 564824
Del Sud - c.so Lodi, 74 - Tel. 530918
De Paris - via Cesare Correnti, 13 - Tel. 877864
Derby Ristorante Club - via Monte Rosa, 84 - Tel. 430027
Des Etrangers - via Sirte, 9 - Tel. 474502
Eden - via Tonale, 2 - Tel. 691609
Eliseo - **via Pecchio, 2 - Tel. 209355**
Emilia - **via Ponte Seveso, 38 - Tel. 600158**
Federale Helvetia - via Polo, 9 - Tel. 664153
Fenice - c.so Buenos Aires, 2 - Tel. 203705
Fiume - via Tenca, 12 - Tel. 662870
Gala - v. Zara, 89 - **Tel. 670867**
Galles - via Ozanam, 1 - Tel. 200625

Garden Hotel - via Rutilia, 6 - Tel. 537368
Ginevra - via Fara, 3 - Tel. 665265
Giulio Cesare - via Rovello, 10 - Tel. 808532
Gran Sasso - via Lippi, 28 - Tel. 296209
Gritti - p. S. Maria Beltrade, 4 - Tel. 800218
Ideale - via S. Spirito, 17 - Tel. 702411
Kent Hotel - via Corridoni, 2/a - Tel. 705173
Liana - via G. Colombo, 14 - Tel. 733943
Ligure e Promessi Sposi - p.za Oberdan, 12 - Tel. 202272
Liguria - via Ripamonti, 134 - Tel. 5391682
London Hotel - via Rovello, 3 - Tel. 807310
Losanna - via Piero della Francesca, 39 - Tel. 316272
Lugano - via Astolfo, 6 - Tel. 293635
Lux - via della Palla, 5 - Tel. 802110
Mac Mahon - via M. Mahon, 45/a - Tel. 332596
Majorca - v. Pellizzone, 12 - Tel. 7384630
Margherita - via S. Gregorio, 30 - Tel. 635260
Mentana - via Morigi, 2 - Tel. 898255
Minerva - c.so Colombo, 15 - Tel. **8480217**
Mistral - v. Toffetti, 4 - Tel. 563197
Monaco - via Cerva, 7 - Tel. 790251
Motel dei Fiori - via Spezia - Tel. 8436441
Motel Tourist - v.le Fulvio Testi, 300 - **Tel. 6437777**
Paganella - via Ghiberti, 31 - Tel. 464059
Park Hotel - via Massena, 9 - Tel. 312525
Parma - via Piero della Francesca, 48 - Tel. 315448
Perugino - via Perugino, 12 - Tel. 576830
Piacenza - via Piacenza, 4 - Tel. 581268
Piccolo Hotel - via Piero della Francesca, 60 - Tel. 340756
Puccini - c. Buenos Aires, 33 - Tel. 220344
Rallye - via Benedetto Marcello, 59 - Tel. 2041957
Rex Hotel - via Marco D'Agrate, 34 - Tel. 533715
Rivoli - via Lulli, 11 - Tel. 226423
Roxy - via Bixio, 6 - Tel. 225409
Salus - via Rossi, 59 - Tel. 6458332
S. Francisco - v.le Lombardia, 55 - Tel. 2361009
San Luca - via Porpora, 48 - Tel. 2365371
Sassonia - via Castaldi, 4 - Tel. 665394
Tonale - via Tonale, 14 - Tel. 691928
Torino - via Caminadella, 11 - Tel. 896220
Trento - via Dal Pozzo Toscanelli, 4 - Tel. 2560758
Union - via Papi, 18 - Tel. 542107
Valganna - via Varè, 32 - Tel. 370089

Vienna - via Astolfo, 5 - Tel. 293251
Virgilio Pier Luigi da Palestrina, 30 - Tel. 200204
Zenit - c. Vercelli, 56 - Tel. 487587

4th Cathegory

Alcione - via Mora, 2 - Tel. 870901
Amalfi - via Quarnero, 18 - Tel. 462478
Argonne - via Labeone, 8 - Tel. 726846
Aurora - via Porpora, 86 - Tel. 293850
Basilea - via Viviani, 2 - Tel. 664732
Bel Sit - via Gallarate, 2 - Tel. 391922
Beretta - via Marghera, 2 - Tel. 495321
Bologna - via Lepetit, 27 - Tel. 201423
Brera - via Pontaccio, 9 - Tel. 873509
Brianza - via Castaldi, 16 - Tel. 265570
Calais - v. Washington, 26 - Tel. 4694760
Calipso - via Gaffurio, 1 - Tel. 203269
Casa Mia - v.le Vitt. Veneto, 30 - Tel. 639006
Castello - via Rovello, 9 - Tel. 807835
Catto - via Pontaccio, 17 - Tel. 807143
Cellini - via Cellini, 24/a - Tel. 795710
Centrale - via Lupetta, 3 - Tel. 890192
Commercio - via Mercato, 1 - Tel. 874921
Correggio - via Correggio, 32 - Tel. 487757
Dateo - v.le Piceno, 33 - Tel. 730857
De Amicis - via De Amicis, 38 - Tel. 877679
Delizia - via Archimede, 88 - Tel. 733638
Del Sole - via Spontini, 6 - Tel. 201871
Doria Suisse - v.le dei Mille, 48 - Tel. 720289
Dover - via Sottocorno, 8 - Tel. 780103
Ferrari - c.so Vercelli, 55 - Tel. 482721
Ginepro & Patria - p.za Cinque Giornate, 6 - Tel. 541468
Ippodromi San Siro - via Pegaso - Tel. 4084294
Lanzone - via Lanzone, 1 - Tel. 800182
Luce - via Strambio, 20 - Tel. 716975
Malta - via Ricordi, 20 - Tel. 208670
Marte - via A. Sforza, 81 - Tel. 8433136
Mazzini - via Vitruvio, 29 - Tel. 279626
Merano - via Lazzaretto, 10 - Tel. 279378
Mignon - via Saronno, 5 - Tel. 381407
Montecarlo - via Vallazze, 39 - Tel. 292427
Montecatini - via Castaldi, 15 - Tel. 664038
Murillo - v.le Murillo, 22/24 - Tel. 432850
Nettuno - via Tadino, 27 - Tel. 200809

Nuovo - p. Beccaria, 6 - Tel. 873205
Paradiso - via B. Marcello, 85 - Tel. 279448
Pavone - via Dandolo, 2 - Tel. 795033
Roma - c. Lodi, 4 - Tel. 541474
Romagna - lg. Rio de Janeiro, 12 - Tel. 292189
Rosalba Hotel - c. Magenta, 22 - Tel. 871763
San Rossore - via Settembrini, 46 - Tel. 279900
S. Marta - via S. Marta, 4 - Tel. 872736
Serena - via Boscovich, 59 - Tel. 200848
Siena - via Castaldi, 17 - Tel. 265674
Speronari - via Speronari, 4 - Tel. 807523
Sport - vl. Monza, 111 - Tel. 280691
Stazione Centrale - p. IV Novembre, 1 - Tel. 691981
Susa - viale Argonne, 14 - Tel. 720897
Trieste e Germania - via Polo, 13 - Tel. 664405
Tripoli - p. Tripoli, 3 - Tel. 470882
Venezia - p. Oberdan, 2/a - Tel. 200797

AMBULANCES

Ambulanza Porta Vittoria - p. 5 Giornate - Tel. 598111
Ambulat. Amici Ambros. Opere P. Pio - v. Doria, 39 -
Tel. 270124
Ambulatorio - v. Rembrandt, 38 - Tel. 4080329
Ambulanza Molise - v. Nicastro, 4 - Tel. 592315
Ambulatorio Croce Azzurra S. Giorgio - v. Inganni, 4 -
Tel. 4155373
Ambulatorio Medico Chirurgico - v. Aselli, 14 - Tel. 730581
Ambulatorio Medico Chirurg. Città Studi - v. Vanvitel-
li, 41 - Tel. 278844
Ambulat. Policl. Medico Chirurg. - v. Fieno, 8 - Tel. 800018
Ambulat. Polispecialistico - v. Bagutta, 12 - Tel. 702708
Chirurg. del Carmine - v. Mercato, 1 - Tel. 807069
Chirurgica P. Magenta - c. Vercelli, 31 - Tel. 482501
Chirurgica S. Siro - v. Monreale, 11 - Tel. 4080216
Croce Verde - p. S. Sepolcro, 9 - Tel. 803800
Porta Venezia (ple Oberdan) - Tel. 228624 - P.ta Ticinese
(p.le XXIV Maggio) - Tel. 8480860 — Staz. Centr. (lato
v. F. Aporti) - Tel. 209521 — Staz. Nord (v. Sassi, 2)
Tel. 867485
Guardia Ostetrica Permanente dell'Asilo Regina Elena -
v. Fanti, 6 - Tel. 541841

CHARITABLE INSTITUTIONS

« La Madunina » - Presidente Molteni Comm. Riccardo - Sede v. Cernaia, 1 - Tel. 662216 - v. Goldoni, 64 - Tel. 712033

Tazzinetta Benefica - v. S. Maria Valle, 2 - Tel. 893959

Salvadanè de la Montagnetta - v. De Amicis, 17 - Tel. 8480672

Dame di Carità S. Vincenzo de Paoli - v. Ariberto, 10 - Tel. 8482667

AUTONOLEGGIO

Autoservizi Maggiore - v. General Fara, 28 - Tel. 664310 Via Canonica, 64 (Direzione) - Tel. 311029

Auto Travel - v. Galvani, 12 - Tel. 680116

A.V.I.S. System - p. Diaz, 6 - Tel. 867622/4 - v. F. Filzi, 43 - Tel. 600516 - Aeroporto Linate - Tel. 717214 - Aeroporto Malpensa - Tel. 868019

CAROP - c.so Sempione, 21 - Tel 341411/15 - Aeroporto Linate - Tel. 7385374

Euroselfdrive - p. della Repubblica, 20 - Tel. 664751/666103

Herts - p. Duca d'Aosta, 7/A - Tel. 652323/437 - Aeroporto Linate - Tel. 7384580 - v. Larga, 20 - Tel. 878591 - Aeroporto Malpensa - Tel. 868001 - via Grazioli, 16 - Tel. 6464156

BANKS

Giorni Feriali 8,30-12,30 - 16-16,45
(Ad eccezione delle seguenti banche: Cassa di Risparmio - Banca del Monte orario continuato 8,30-13,45)
Sabato e giorni festivi chiuso

Banca Agricola Milanese - v. Mazzini, 9/11 - Tel. 8809

Banca American Express Bank - v. Monte di Pietà, 11 - Tel. 8690551

Banca Belinzaghi - v. Andegari, 14 - Tel. 8826

Banca Cesare Ponti - p. Duomo ,19 - Tel. 8821

Banca Chase Manhattan Bank - p. Meda, 1 - Tel. 8895

Banca Commerciale Italiana - p. Scala, 6 - 8850

Banca Commercio Industria - v. Moscova, 33 - Tel. 6275

Banca Coppola G. - v. T. Grossi, 2 - Tel. 890960

Banca d'America e d'Italia - v. Manzoni, 5 - Tel. 8827

Banca del Monte di Milano v. Monte di Pietà, 7 Tel. 8886

Banca di Credito di Milano - v. Mengoni, 2 - Tel. 898542

Banca di Legnano - v. Rovello, 12 - Tel. 876744

Banca d'Italia - v. Cordusio, 5 - Tel. 861892
Banca Generale di Credito - v. Borromei, 5 - Tel. 8867
Banca Hambros Bank Limited - p. S. Fedele, 2 - Tel. 865157
Banca Italo Israeliana - v. Manzoni, 5/a - Tel. 807551
Banca Lombarda Dep. e c/c - v. S. Pellico, 10 - Tel. 800311
Banca Loria & C. - p. P. Ferrari, 8 - Tel. 879441
Banca Manusardi & C. - v. Broletto, 37 - Tel. 870051
Banca Mediobanca - v. Filodrammatici, 10 - Tel. 8829
Banca Milanese di Credito - p. Belgioioso, 2 - Tel. 793146
Banca Monte Paschi di Siena - v. S. Margherita, 11 - Tel. 8806
Banca Morgan Vonwiller - v. Armorari, 14 - Tel. 876941
Banca Mutua Pop. Agric. di Lodi - v. Larga, 31 - Tel. 865356
Banza Naz. delle Comunicazioni - p. IV Novembre - Tel. 266703
Banca Nazionale del Lavoro - p. S. Fedele, 1/3 - Tel. 8853
Banca Nazionale dell'Agricoltura - p. Fontana, 4 - Tel. 8894
Banca Piccolo Cred. Bergamasco - v. Orsole, 4 - Tel. 862141
Banca Popolare di Crema - v. Tazzoli, 11 - Tel. 669664
Banca Popolare di Abbiategrasso - v. Merlo, 1 - Tel. 790135
Banca Popolare di Bergamo - v. Boito, 5 - Tel. 860741
Banca Popolare di Lecco - v. dei Mercanti, 10 - Tel. 8690451
Banca Popolare di Lodi - v. Larga, 31 - Tel. 865356
Banca Pop. Luino e Varese - v. Camperio, 3 - Tel. 867441
Banca Popolare di Milano - p. Meda, 2/4 - Tel. 7725
Banca Popolare di Novara - v. S. Protaso, 8 - Tel. 8848
Banca Privata Finanziaria - v. Verdi, 7 - Tel. 8893
Banca Privata Milanese - v. Clerici, 1 - Tel. 876145
Banca Provinc. Depositi e Sconti - v. Verdi, 3 - Tel. 808929
Banca Provinciale Lombarda - p. Diaz, 7 - Tel. 8860
Banca Rasini - v. dei Mercanti, 5 - Tel. 862541
Banca Rosenberg Colorni Candiani - v. Verdi, 4 - Tel. 896354
Banca S. Paolo - Brescia - 4. v. G. Negri - Tel 872575
Banca Subalpina - v. Manzoni, 9 - Tel. 808141
Banca Unione - v. S. Maria Segreta, 5 - Tel. 803853
Banco Ambrosiano - v. Clerici, 2 - Tel. 8837
Banco Lariano - v. Hoepli, 10 - 890251
Banco di Napoli - p. Cordusio - Tel. 8804
Banco di Roma - p. T. Edison, 1 - Tel. 8863
Banco di Sicilia - v. S. Margherita, 12/14 - Tel. 8849
Banco Fratelli Tolja & C. - p. S. Maria Beltrade, 1 - Tel. 896157
Bank of America Nt & Sa - v. Verdi, 2 - Tel. 864262
Banque Nationale de Paris - v. Boito, 10 - Tel. 865391

Cassa di Risparmio Provincie Lombarde - v. **Monte di Pie**-tà, 8 - Tel. **8866**
Cassa Lombarda - v. Manzoni, 14 - Tel. 894341
Castellini C. & Co. - v. Giulini, 4 - Tel. 800955
Comp. Finanz. Mob. - v. Monte di Pietà, 15 - Tel. 808696
Centrobanca - c. Europa, 18 - Tel. 780331
Credit Commercial de France - p. M. Bossi, 1 - Tel. 800879
Credito Agrario Bresciano - p. Borromeo, 1 - Tel. 802382
Credito Artigiano - p. S. Fedele, 4 - Tel. 896343
Credito Commerciale - v. Armorari, 4 - Tel. 8824
Credito Italiano - p. Cordusio, 2 - Tel. 8862
Credito Lombardo - v. S. Pietro All'Orto, 24 - Tel. 7736
Credito Varesino - v. Bassano Porrone, 6 - Tel. 8814
Efibanca - v. Meravigli, 18 - Tel. 800771
First National City Bank - p. Repubblica, 2 - Tel. 6253
Fiscambi - p. Diaz, 7 - Tel. 866841
Interbanca - v. Montenapoleone, 23 - Tel. 781454
Istituto Bancario Italiano - v. Manzoni, 3 - Tel. 8890
Istit. Banc. S. Paolo di Torino - v. Broletto, **9 - Tel. 8808**
Istit. Centrale delle Banche Popolari Italiane - c. **Europa**, 18 - Tel. 708241
Istit. Centrale Banche e Banchieri - v. Boito, 8 - Tel. 803230
Istit. Mobiliare Italiano - p. S. Fedele, 2 - Tel. 862257
Itabanca - Soc. Ital. Credito - p. Mercanti, 11 - Tel. 803771
Mediocredito Region. Lombardo - v. Broletto, 20 - **Tel. 8870**

CHAMBERS OF COMMERCE

Camera Confed. del Lavoro di Milano e **Provincia - c.so** P. Vittoria, 43 - Tel. 793950
C. di C. Industria Artigianato e Agricoltura - v. Meravigli, 9-B - Tel. 8854
C. di C. Americana per l'Italia - v. Agnello, 12 - Tel. 807955
C. di C. Britannica per l'Italia - v. Tarchetti, 1/3 - Tel. 635860
C. di C. dell'Iran per l'Italia - p. Repubblica, 10 - Tel. 651580
C. di C. Industria Italo-Belga - v. Mascheroni, **2 - Tel.** 874441
C. di C. Francese per l'Italia - v. Meravigli, **12 - Tel. 893890**
C. di C. Ital. Parigi - v. Beatrice d'Este, 4 - Tel. 8480557
C. di C. Ital. per Scambi Inter. - v. Jan, 18 - Tel. 269228
C. di C. Italiana Sud Africa - v. del Bollo, 5 - Tel. 860932
C. di C. Ital. Cecoslovacchia - v. Albricci, 3 - Tel. 861167

C. di C. Italiana per la Gran Bretagna e il Commonwealth - c. Venezia, 8 - Tel. 793536
C. di C. Italiana per l'estero - v. Manzoni, 42 - Tel. 792700
C. di C. Italo-Argentina - v. Mascheroni, 5 - Tel. 431400
C. di C. Italo-Austriaca - v. S. Radegonda, 11 - Tel. 873141
C. di C. Italo-Brasiliana - c. Matteotti, 7 - Tel. 709972
C. di C. Italo-Centro America - v. Terraggio, 17 - Tel. 898070
C. di C. Italo-Egiziana - v. Manzoni, 21 - Tel. 860697
C. di C. Italo-Germanica - v. Torriani, 29 - Tel. 652651
C. di C. Italo-Indonesiana - v. Battisti, 2 - Tel. 790983
C. di C. Italo-Iraniana - vl. Papiniano, 28 - Tel. 4691845
C. di C. Italo-Israeliana - v. Romagnosi, 1 - Tel. 873000
C. di C. Italo-Jugoslava - v. Cernaia, 9 - Tel. 650861
C. di C. Italo-Olandese - v. S. Vittore, 45 - Tel. 4930581
C. di C. Italo-Pakistana - v. Tunisia, 48 - Tel. 669667
C. di C. Italo-Sovietica - v. Fatebenefratelli, 4 - Tel. 864301
C. di C. Norvegese in Italia - p. Castello, 20 - Tel. 870083
C. di C. Spagnola in Italia - v. Rugabella, 1 - Tel. 861137
C. di C. Svizzera in Italia - v. Palestro, 2 - Tel. 794475

CENTRI COMMERCIALI

AMERICANO - v. Gattamelata, 5 - Tel. 4696451
COREANO - v. Camperio, 1 - Tel. 876806
DELLA REPUBBLICA DELLA CINA (di Formosa) - v. F. Filzi, 2 - Tel. 635.070

UFFICI COMMERCIALI DI:

AUSTRIA PER IL COMM. EST. - p. Duomo, 20 - Tel. 866123
BULGARIA - v. G. Fara, 20 - Tel. 664276
CANADA' - v. Vittor Pisani, 19 - Tel. 6526000
CUBA - Via Turati, 3 - Tel. 632768
FINLANDIA - v. Camperio, 9 - Tel. 892800
FRANCIA - v. Cusani, 10 - Tel. 871575
GOVERNO DELL'ONTARIO - v. Senato, 12 - Tel. 781162
GRECIA - v. Cornalia, 24 - Tel. 664779
POLONIA - v. Camperio, 1 - Tel. 878692-3-4-5
PORTOGHESE - v. Camperio, 1 - Tel. 874910
PROVINCIA DI QUEBEC - v. Manzoni, 16 - Tel. 795673
REPUBBLICA POP. D'ALBANIA - v. Larga, 2 - Tel. 867393
REPUB. SOC. CECOSLOVACCA - c. B. Aires, 79 - Tel. 220741
ROMANIA - v. Orti, 3 - Tel. 553434
SUD AFRICA - v. Q. Sella, 4 - Tel. 803478
DELEGAZIONE DELLA CAMERA DI COMMERCIO ITALIANA DI PARIGI - v. Meravigli, 16 - Tel. 808019

RAPP. DELLA CAMERA DI COMM. ESTERO DELLA REP.
TEDESCA - v. Pier Lombardo, 30 - Tel. 5460016
SEZIONE ECONOMICA DELL'AMBASCIATA DI INDONE-
SIA - v. Podgora, 1 - Tel. 794787
UNGHERESE - v. Boccaccio, 18 - Tel. 876017

CAMPINGS AND YOUTH HOSTELS

AGIP - S. Donato Milanese - camping AGIP - Tel. 5272159
Autodromo di Monza Parco Villa Reale - Tel. 22366
Campeggio Città di Milano - v. Pienza, 1 - Tel. 8497794
Riviera di Milano - Idroscalo - Tel. 717492
Ostello per la Gioventù A.I.G. Piero Rotta - v. Salmoira-
ghi, 2 - Tel. 367095

CASE - ALBERGO

Apartment House « Le Gazzelle » - v. Cavezzali, 11 - Tel.
2893685
Casa - Albergo - v. Finocchiaro Aprile, 2 - Tel. 662056
Casa - Albergo - v. Zarotto, 8 - Tel. 637.579
Casa - Albergo Bassini - v. Bassini, 36 - Tel. 292340
Casa - Albergo - v. Corridoni, 22 - Tel. 793.364
Casa - Albergo di Via Giusti - v. Alberti, 6 - Tel. 335844
Casa - Albergo Habitat - v. Tolstoi - Tel. 474491
Casa - Albergo Missori - v. Albricci, 2 - Tel. 8857
Casa della Laureata - v. Respighi, 8
Casa Svizzera - v. S. Raffaele, 3 - Tel. 807738
Domus Patrizia - v. Pier Lombardo, 20 - Tel. 592478
Due Torri Residence - v. Fara, 26/a - Tel. 635201
Glory Residence - v. Pola, 4 - Tel. 690444
La Residenza - v. Scialoia, 3 - Tel. 6461646
Pfeiffer International House - v. Aldini, 9 - Tel. 3554546
Principessa Clotilde Residence - c.so Porta Nuova, 52 -
Tel. 6243
Residence - c.so Italia, 34 - Tel. 806546
Residence 5 - p.za S. Stefano, 5 - Tel. 867531
Residence della Corsia - c.so Vitt. Emanuele, 8 - Tel. 782151
Residence Elite - c.so Europa, 9 - Tel. 7743
Residence Garden - v. Salvioni, 6 - Tel. 341949
Residence Gran Sasso - v. Garofalo, 32 - Tel. 221251
Residence House - v. Palazzi, 20 - Tel. 221098
Residence Milano Sud - v. Momigliano, 2 - Tel. 8434951
Residence Sette Cupole - v. Nievo, 33 - Tel. 315941
Residence Villa Magentina Heby - v. Bertieri, 2 - Tel. 4229497

CINEMAS, THEATRES

Teatri
Alla Scala - p.zza Scala - Tel. 8879
Angelicum - S. Angelo, 2 - Tel. 632748
Arte - Palazzo Triennale - v.le Alemagna, 6 - Tel. 865469
Colibri - v. Valpetrosa, 5 - Tel. 874826
Conservatorio - v. Conservatorio, 12 - Tel. 701755
Club D'Essai - via dei Chiostri, 8 - Tel. 435848
Filodrammatici - v. Filodrammatici, 1 - Tel. 803656
Gerolamo - p.zza Beccaria - Tel. 871422
La Commenda - v. Curtatone - tel. 545200
Litta - c.so Magenta, 25 - Tel. 861939
Lirico - via Larga, 14 - Tel. 866418
Manzoni - via Manzoni, 42 - Tel. 790545
Maschere - via Borgogna, 7 - Tel. 705584
Nuovo - c.so Vittorio Emanuele, 37 - Tel. 700088
Odeon - S. Radegonda, 8 - Tel. 876320
Piccola Scala - via Filodrammatici - Tel. 8879
Piccolo Teatro - via Rovello, 2 - Tel. 872352
Puccini - c.so Buenos Ayres - Tel. 276793
San Babila - corso Venezia, 2 - Tel. 702985
San Marco - piazza S. Marco, 2 - Tel. 639156
Smeraldo - p.zza XXV Aprile, 12 - Tel. 662768
Uomo - c.so Manusardi, 7 - Tel. 835665

Cinema PRIME VISIONI
Alcione - p.zza Vetra, 1 - Tel. 873597
Ambasciatori - c.so V. Emanuele - Tel. 709306
Angelicum - S. Angelo - Tel. 661712
Apollo - c.so Vitt. Emanuele, 7-2 - Tel. 780390
Ariston - Galleria Corso, 1 - Tel. 793806
Arlecchino Cin. d'Essai - S. Pietro all'Orto, 9 - Tel. 701214
Arti - via Mascagni, 8 - Tel. 790048
Capitol - via Croce Rossa - Tel. 637067
Cavour - p.zza Cavour, 3 - Tel. 635779
Corso - Galleria Corso, 1 - Tel. 702184
Durini - via Durini, 23 - Tel. 793314
Eden - via Beltrami, 1 - Tel. 802408
Excelsior - Galleria Corso - Tel. 702354
Manzoni - via Manzoni, 40 - Tel. 790650
Mediolanum - c.so Vitt. Emanuele, 24 - Tel. 790818
Metro Astra - c.so V. Emanuele - Tel. 700229
Mignon - Galleria del Corso, 4 - 792343
Missori - p.zza Missori, 1 - Tel. 807325

Odeon - S. Radegonda, 10 - Tel. 874547
Ritz Cinema d'Essai - via Torino, 21 - Tel. 890771
Rivoli - via Cerva, 35 - Tel. 793379

PROSEGUIMENTO PRIME

Arcadia - c.so P.ta Romana, 65 - Tel. 540726
Astor - c.so Buenos Aires, 36 - Tel. 270670
Atlas - via Sansovino, 3 - Tel. 279122
Aurora - via P. Sarpi, 6 - Tel. 341305
Cielo - v.le Premuda, 46 - Tel. 798468
Colosseo - via Montenero, 84 - Tel. 553361
Dal Verme - S. G. sul Muro - Tel. 871638
De Amicis - via De Amicis, 34 - Tel. 899240
Diamante - via F. Filzi, 5 - Tel. 637952
Diana - viale Piave, 42 - Tel. 220910
Eliseo - via Torino, 64 - Tel. 802752
Gloria - c.so Vercelli, 18 - Tel. 482347
Golden - v. Cagliero, 14/A - Tel. 6888146
Impero - via Vitruvio, 10 - Tel. 221464
Mercury - c.so P. Romana, 124 - Tel. 553547
Metropol - v.le Piave, 24 - Tel. 799913
Paris - C.so Garibaldi, 99 - Tel. 665534
Piccolo Eden - via Beltrami, 1 - Tel. 802408
Plinius - v.le Abruzzi, 28 - Tel. 225103
Puccini - corso Buenos Aires - Tel. 276793
Tiziano - via Cassiodoro, 12 - Tel. 430130
Tonale - via Tonale, 3 - Tel. 6086657
X Cine Nuovo - via Menotti, 11 - Tel. 716791
Zenit - p.za Piemonte, 2 - Tel. 482155

CINE D'ESSAI

Anteo - via Milazzo, 9 - Tel. 637732
Orchidea - via Terraggio, 3 - Tel. 875389
Rubino - via Soncino, 3 - Tel. 875006

SECONDE VISIONI

Alce - via Caposile, 5 - Tel. 585571
Alexander - via Palmanova, 75 - Tel. 287959
Ambrosiano - corso XXII Marzo, 32 - Tel. 733172
America - via Tito Livio, 2 - Tel. 540717
Arcobaleno - viale Tunisia, 11 - Tele. 266054
Argentina - piazza Argentina, 4 - Tel. 222186
Augusteo - via Sarpi, 52 - Tel. 389688
Eolo - via Mac Mahon, 16 - Tel. 347679

La Fenice - via Bligny, 52 - Tel. 592367
Las Vegas, via Meda, 49 - Tel. 8493975
Massimo - via E. Torricelli, 2 - Tel. 8484264
Meravigli - via Meravigli, 3 - Tel. 806361
Nazionale - piazza Piemonte - Tel. 431700
Orfeo - C. Zugna, 50 - Tel. 833039
Poliziano - via Poliziano, 11 - Tel. 381505
Roma - via Piatti, 1 - Tel. 897322
Roxi - corso Lodi, 158 - Tel. 538468
Splendor - via Donatello, 37 - Tel. 2365124

VISIONI ULTERIORI

Abadan - via Busoni, 9 - Tel. 541861
Abanella - via Bottelli, 11 - Tel. 683752
A.B.C. - viale Monza, 101 - Tel. 286749
Adriano - via Gulli, 7 - Tel. 4080208
Adua - via Monte Oliveto, 6 - Tel. 503559
Alfieri - via Imbonati, 27 - Tel. 600227
Alpi - via Ricciarelli, 11 - Tel. 4080607
Araldo - via Lorenteggio, 208 - Tel. 419497
Aramis - via Padova, 272 - Tel. 2560553
Argo - viale Monza, 79 - Tel. 2899766
Ariosto - via Ariosto, 16 - Tel. 496901
Astoria - v.le Montenero, 55 - Tel. 598424
Boston - p.zza Angilberto, 10 - Tel. 560427
Bruzzano - Via Casarsa, 13 - Tel. 6452950
Centrale - via Torino, 30 - Tel. 874826
Cinestazione - Staz. Centrale - Tel. 209244
Cittanova - via Giambellino, 153 - Tel. 4155295
Continental - via Pier Lombardo, 16 - Tel. 584410
Cristallo - via Castelbarco, 13/a - Tel. 830176
Dea - via Sangallo, 33 - Tel. 730021
Delle Stelle - via Lambro, 14 - Tel. 203996
Derby - via Ripamonti, 170 - Tel. 530382
Donizetti - via Masolino da Panicale, 13 - Tel. 391051
Ducale - piazza Napoli, 27 - Tel. 470991
Duse - via Varè, 73 - Tel. 370672
Embassy - via Faa Di Bruno, 8 - Tel. 573044
Europa - via Binda, 4 - Tel. 479611
Fossati - Garibaldi, 15 - Tel. 872379
Gardenia - via Forze Armate, 338 - Tel. 4090277
Giada - via Galeno, 25 - Tel. 2574047
Giardini - via Vittorio Veneto, 2 - Tel. 221873

Gnomo - via Lanzone 30-a - Tel. 861874
Hermes - via Daniele Crespi, 14 - Tel. 833324
Ideal - corso Lodi, 6 - Tel. 576101
Imperia - via Ornato, 10 - Tel. 6421571
Italia - corso Lodi, 39 - Tel. 576438
Jolly - corso Colombo, 13 - Tel. 8473386
Loreto - p.le Loreto - Tel. 2892563
Magenta - via Sanzio, 23 - Tel. 463348
Marconi - S. Gregorio, 46 - Tel. 637033
Mexico - via Savona, 57 - Tel. 479802
Minerva - via Crema, 2 - Tel. 576232
Modena - via S. Gregorio, 3 - Tel. 221576
Museo Scienza e Tecnica - S. Vittore, 21 - Tel. 462709
Nobel - via A. Sforza, 81 - Tel. 8493746
Perla - via Imbriani, 19 - Tel. 371026
Piccadilly - P. Rossi, 80 - Tel. 6450612
Porpora - via Porpora, 104 - Tel. 230385
Rialto - via Mulino Armi, 47 - Tel. 833663
Rosa - via Canonica, 51 - Tel. 341684
Rossini - via Mambretti, 25 - Tel. 3570511
Sempione - via Pacinotti, 6 - Tel. 322124
Susa - via Giovanni da Milano, 16 - Tel. 720078
Universal - Trezzano s/ Naviglio - Tel. 4451860
Venezia - c.so Buenos Aires, 39
XXII Marzo - c.so XXII Marzo, 14 - Tel. 598934
Vox - via Farini, 30 - Tel. 691808
Zara - via Garigliano, 10 - Tel. 6882339
Zodiaco - via Padova, 179 - Tel. 2563050

CLINICS   HOSPITALS
A.N.E.A. - v. Saint Bon, 3 - Tel. 4080484
Ansaldo - v. S. Canzio, 4 - Tel. 200588
Bassi A. - v. Livigno, 3 - Tel. 694754
Bassini - v. Ricordi, 1 - Tel. 2041251
Capitanio - v. Mercalli, 30 - Tel. 5888551
Casa di Cura « S. Camillo » - v. Macchi, 5 - Tel. 2041551

Casa di Cura San Giovanni - v. Civitali, 71 - Tel. 4087165
Casa di Cura S. Giuseppe - v. S. Vittore, 12 - Tel. 861941
Centro Ortop. Traumat. v. Vincenzo da Seregno, 39 Tel. 6402
Chirurgico Ronzoni G. - v. G. Ronzoni, 1 - Tel. 8488751
Città di Milano - v. Lamarmora, 10 - Tel. 559151
Clinica del Lavoro L. Devoto - v. S. Barnaba, 8 - Tel. 576091
Clinica Dermosifilopatica dell'Univ. di Milano - C.A.V.E. -
  v. della Pace, 9 - Tel. 5460744
Clin. Istituto di Angiologia e di Chirurgia Vascolare - v. del-
  la Commenda, 10 - Tel. 584741
Clin. Istituto di Chirurgia Plastica Ricostruttiva - v. della
  Commenda, 10 - Tel. 584741
Clinica Istituto Ospitaliero Provinciale per la Maternità
  (I.O.P.M.) - v. Melloni, 52 - Tel. 723291
Clinica Istituto Provinciale di Protezione ed Assistenza In-
  fanzia (I.P.P.A.I.) - vl. Piceno, 60 - Tel. 723051
Clin. Ist. di Puericultura - v. Commenda, 9 - Tel. 544541
Clinica Morgagni - v. Calvi, 22 - Tel. 793456
Clinica Oculistica - v. della Commenda, 16 - Tel. 598849
Clinica Oculistica - v. F. Sforza, 35 - Tel. 542448
Clinica Odontoiatrica - v. della Commenda, 10 - Tel. 584741
Clin. Ostetrica Ginecologica L. Mangiagalli - v. della Com-
  menda, 12 - Tel. 593341
Clinica Otorinolaringologica - v. Commenda, 16 - Tel. 542463
Clinica Pediatrica G. e D. De Marchi - v. della Commenda, 9
  Tel. 544541
Clinica Padiglione Polichirurgico Alfieri - v. della Commen-
  da, 12 - Tel. 584741
Clinica Psichiatrica Univ. di Mil. - v. Besta, 1 - Tel. 6453167
Columbus - v. Buonarroti, 48 - Tel. 495946
Croce Rossa Italiana « Principessa Jolanda » - v. Carados-
  so, 9 - Tel. 892855
Del Policlinico - v. Dezza, 48 - Tel. 4692641
Della Cassa Edile - v. S. Luca, 6 - Tel. 8486151
Fatebenefratelli - c.so Porta Nuova, 23 - Tel. 654941
Felix - v. Sanremo, 9 - Tel. 720074
Fitoterapia Pesce - v. Monterosa, 88 - Tel. 4692934
Igea - v. Marcona, 69 - Tel. 7382951
Istituti Clinici di Perfezion. - v. Commenda, 12 - Tel. 593341
Istituto Naz. per lo Studio e la Cura dei Tumori - v. Ve-
  nezian, 1 - Tel. 2363940
Istituto Neurologico C. Besta -v. Celoria, 11 - Tel. 2364273
Istituto Oftalmico - v. Castelfidardo - Tel. 667416

Istituto Ortop. Elioterapico - p. A. Ferrari, 4 - Tel. 5460484
Istituto Ortopedico G. Pini - vl. Monza, 223 - Tel. 2572812
Istituto Ortop. Gaetano Pini - p. A. Ferrari, 1 - Tel. 5494
Istituti Ospitalieri di Milano - p. Ospedale Magg., 3 - Telefono 6420812 - v. F. Sforza, 35 - Tel. 581655
Istituto Ospitaliero Provinc. P. Pini di Affori - Tel. 645164
Istit. Stomatologico Italiano - v. Commenda, 19 - Tel. 581951
Istituto Stomatologico Italiano - v. Pace
La Madonnina - v. Quadronno, 29 - Tel. 593541
Le Quattro Marie - v. Bonfadini, 214 - Tel. 5090
Maggiore Ca' Granda (Niguarda) - v. Ospedale Maggiore, 3 - Tel. 6444
Maggiore S. Carlo - v. Pio II, 3 - Tel. 4022
Maria Ausiliatrice - v. Rogoredo, 31 - Tel. 510142
Militare - via Saint Bon, 5 - Tel. 457081
Ospedale dei Bambini Vittore Buzzi - v. Castelvetro, 32 - Tel. 381041
Pio Istituto Santa Corona - c.so Italia, 52 - Tel. 8394941
Policlinico - v. F. Sforza, 28 - Tel. 8820
Regina Elena - Istit. Ostetrico, Ginecologico e Pediatrico - v. M. Fanti, 6 - Tel. 541841
Sanatoriale L. Sacco (Vialba) - v. Grassi, 74 - Tel. 3556345
Sant'Ambrogio - v. Faravelli, 16 - Tel. 344651
Sant'Anna - v. Donizetti, 14 - Tel. 790091
S. Carlo - v. Lombardo, 22 - Tel. 544531
S. Caterina - v. Commenda, 12 - Tel. 584741
S. Pio X - v. Nava, 31 - Tel. 6884741
Santa Rita - v. Catalani, 18 - Tel. 293606
S. Siro - v. Monreale, 18 - Tel. 4034341
Salus - v. Ruggero di Lauria, 2 - Tel. 384741
SANATRIX - v. Jommelli, 15 - Tel. 296501
Villa Aegla - v. Spagnoletto, 3 - Tel. 432790
Villa Porpora - v. Carpi, 30 - Tel. 230457
Villa Turro - v. Prinetti, 29 - Tel. 287185

CODICI POSTALI
E DISTANZE CHILOMETRICHE DA MILANO

92100	AGRIGENTO	1685	75100	MATERA	939
15100	ALESSANDRIA	95	98100	MESSINA	1395
60100	ANCONA	427	41100	MODENA	179
11100	AOSTA	187	80100	NAPOLI	831
52100	AREZZO	402	28100	NOVARA	47
63100	ASCOLI PICENO	546	08100	NUORO	866
14100	ASTI	118	35100	PADOVA	242
83100	AVELLINO	858	90100	PALERMO	1660
70100	BARI	915	43100	PARMA	126
32100	BELLUNO	318	27100	PAVIA	35
82100	BENEVENTO	825	06100	PERUGIA	461
24100	BERGAMO	50	61100	PESARO - URBINO	365
40100	BOLOGNA	218	65100	PESCARA	576
39100	BOLZANO	268	29100	PIACENZA	67
25100	BRESCIA	92	56100	PISA	290
72100	BRINDISI	1029	51100	PISTOIA	304
09100	CAGLIARI	1059	33170	PORDENONE	327
93100	CALTANISSETTA	1628	85100	POTENZA	934
86100	CAMPOBASSO	782	97100	RAGUSA	1596
81100	CASERTA	813	48100	RAVENNA	296
95100	CATANIA	1492	89100	REGGIO CAL.	1395
88100	CATANZARO	1254	42100	REGGIO EMILIA	147
66100	CHIETI	593	02100	RIETI	571
22100	COMO	43	00100	ROMA	613
87100	COSENZA	1166	45100	ROVIGO	250
26100	CREMONA	85	84100	SALERNO	878
12100	CUNEO	225	07100	SASSARI	868
94100	ENNA	1591	17100	SAVONA	189
44100	FERRARA	246	53100	SIENA	391
50100	FIRENZE	325	96100	SIRACUSA	1568
71100	FOGGIA	788	23100	SONDRIO	134
47100	FORLI'	282	74100	TARANTO	992
03100	FROSINONE	711	64100	TERAMO	564
16100	GENOVA	149	05100	TERNI	543
34170	GORIZIA	408	10100	TORINO	144
58100	GROSSETO	437	91100	TRAPANI	1764
18100	IMPERIA	260	38100	TRENTO	208
86019	ISERNIA	726	31100	TREVISO	275
67100	L'AQUILA	631	34100	TRIESTE	415
19100	LA SPEZIA	234	33100	UDINE	368
04100	LATINA	698	21100	VARESE	51
73100	LECCE	1063	30100	VENEZIA	283
57100	LIVORNO	311	13100	VERCELLI	70
55100	LUCCA	289	37100	VERONA	159
62100	MACERATA	472	36100	VICENZA	209
46100	MANTOVA	153	01100	VITERBO	537
54100	MASSA CARRARA	246			

SHIPPING AND AIRWAYS COMPANIES

Aer Lingus - Linee Aeree Irlandesi - v. Gonzaga, 7 - Telefono 893042

Aerolineas Argentinas - v. Albricci, 9 - Tel. 898929

Aeronaves de Mexico - v. Cesariano, 10 - Tel. 346897

Aero Servizi Internazionali - v. G. Fara, 28 - Tel. 666550

Agamare Milano - v. del Politecnico, 3 - Tel. 798269

Agenzia Generale Traghetti Canguro - v. V. Pisani, 13 - Telefono 667449

Agenzia Gen. Traghetti Canguro - v. Pisani, 13 - Tel. 653951

Air Afrique - v. Turati, 6 - Tel. 667575

Air Canada - p.za Missori, 3 - Tel. 8690704

Air Congo - v. Cesariano, 7 - Tel. 339823

Air-France - p.za Cavour, 2 - Tel. 798241

Air India - p.za Diaz, 5 - Tel. 860565/871697

Alisarda c/o SEA Viaggi - p.za Duca d'Aosta 7/A - Telefono 654302

Alitalia - v. Albricci, 5 - Tel. 6989 - Air Terminal - v. Galvani, 12 - Tel. 6988 - Aeroporto Linate - Tel. 7395

ARMEC - v. Borgonuovo, 11 - Tel. 8690431

Austrian Airlines - v. Albricci, 7 - Tel. 807357

Avianca - Linee Aeree Colombiane - p.za Velasca, 5 - Telefono 898830

B.E.A. - British European Airways - p.za Diaz, 7 - Teletono 877841

Canadian Pacific Airlines - v. U. Foscolo, 1 - Tel. 870658

Costa - Compagnia di Navigazione - Foro Bonaparte, 71 - Telefono 866912/896245

El-Al - Linee Aeree Israeliane - v. Larga, 31 - Tel. 806500

Ethiopian Airlines - v. Paolo da Cannobio, 33 - Tel. 896562

Finnair - Linee Aeree Finlandesi - v. Albricci, 5 - Tel. 864265

Flotta Lauro - v. Palestro, 6 - Tel. 704812

Iberia - Linee Aeree Spagnole - v. Albricci, 8 - Tel. 8899

Iran Air - v. Albricci, 10 - Tel. 879270

Italia - Comp. Navig. Lloyd Triestino - Adriatica - v. Case Rotte, 5 - Tel. 860651 - Tirrenia 862540/570

Itavia - p.za Duca d'Aosta, 10 - Tel. 202800

JAL - Japan Air Lines - v. Albricci, 10 - Tel. 877069

Jat - Linee Aeree Jugoslave - v. Agnello, 18 - Tel. 807141

K.L.M. - v. Paolo da Cannobio, 33 - Tel. 899841

Linee Aeree Cecoslovacche - v. P. da Cannobio, 5 - Telefono 8690246

LOT - Linee Aeree Polacche - v. Albricci, 9 - Tel. 895897
Lufthansa - Linee Aeree Germaniche - v. Larga, 23 - Telefono 879141
Malev - Linee Aeree Ungheresi - v. Colonna, 49 - Tel. 464779
M.E.A. - Middle East Airlines Airliban - v. Albricci, 9 - Telefono 870278
Olympic Airways - Linee Aeree Greche - p.za Missori, 3 - Tel. 873170
Pakistan International Airlines - v. Paolo da Cannobio, 16 - Tel. 867773
Pan American World Airways - p.za Velasca, 5 - Tel. 877241
Qantas - Linee Aeree Australiane - p.za Diaz, 7 - Tel. 803560
Royal Air Maroc - v. Turati, 8 - Tel. 652418
Sabena - Linee Aeree Belghe - v. Albricci, 7 - Tel. 876787
S.A.M. - Società Aerea Mediterranea - v. Unione, 3 - Telefono 897583
S.A.S. - Scandinavian Airlines System - v. Albricci, 7 - Telefono 867541
Seaboard World Airlines - p. Liberty, 8 - Tel. 706927
SIMA - International Airlines Services - v. Cesariano, 7 Tel. 346897
South African Airways - v. M. Gonzaga, 3 - Tel. 804779
Swissair - v. Vittor Pisani, 31 - Tel. 669141
Tunis Air - Linee Aeree Tunisine - v. Agnello, 8 - Tel. 897752
T.W.A - Trans World Air-line - c.so Europa, 9/11 - Telefono 794653/6
United Arab Airlines - v. Larga, 26 - Tel. 865777
Varig - Linee Aeree Brasiliane - v. Larga, 26 - Tel. 878921
Viasa - Linee Aeree Venezuelane - v. Paolo da Cannobio, 33 - Zim (Comp. navig. israeliana) - v. Agnello, 20 - Tel. 803221

CONSULATES

Argentina - v. Meravigli, 12 - Tel. 864185
Australia - v. Turati, 40 - Tel. 665255
Austria - v. Mascheroni, 25 - Tel. 482066
Belgio - v. A. Vespucci, 2 - Tel. 669479
Bolivia - v. Monferrato, 13 - Tel. 4980130
Brasile - c.so G. Matteotti, 7 - Tel. 793762
Canada - v. Pisani, 19 - Tel. 652600
Cecoslovacchia - c.so Buenos Aires, 79 - Tel. 220526
Cile - v. dei Gradenigo, 3 - Tel. 4075976
Cina (di Formosa) - p. Repubblica, 25/7 - Tel. 652134

Cipro - p. Gobetti, 12 - Tel. 235913
Colombia - p. Repubblica, 32 - **Tel.** 654023
Costarica - v. Maino, 17/a - Tel. 705602
Danimarca - v. de Amicis, 61 - **Tel.** 8484485
Del Madagascar - c. Venezia, 42 - **Tel.** 799293
El Salvador - c. Venezia, 24 - **Tel.** 794633
Filippine - v. Caradosso, 18 - Tel. 871739
Finlandia - v. Bigli, 3 - Tel. 701156
Francia - v. Vecchio Politecnico, 3 - Tel. 798178
Gabon - v. Bigli, 26 - Tel. 790764
Germania - v. Solferino, 40 - **Tel.** 635461
Giappone - p. Diaz, 7 - **Tel.** 867559
Gran Bretagna - v. S. **Paolo,** 7 - **Tel.** 803442
Grecia - v. Turati, 6 - Tel. **638624**
Guatemala - v. Alberto da Giussano, 26 - Tel. 495388
Haiti - p. Duomo, 19 - Tel. 808609
Honduras - p.tta Guastalla, 10 - **Tel.** 794370
Iran - p. della Repubblica, 10 - **Tel.** 650888
Islanda - v. Donatello, 21 - **Tel.** 273010
Israele - c. Europa, 12 - Tel. 705477
Jugoslavia - v. Pirandello, 3 - Tel. 482019
Kuwait - p. Cavour, 3 - **Tel.** 651066
Libano - v. Larga, 26 - Tel. 890345
Liberia - v. s. Agnese, 3 - **Tel.** 872271
Libia - p. del Duomo, 22 - **Tel.** 878457
Lussemburgo - p. Sempione, 4 **Tel.** 389162
Malta - p. Missori, 2 - **Tel.** 891877
Messico - v. Cappuccini, 4 - Tel. 790541
Monaco - v. Brera, 12 - **Tel.** 872868
Nicaragua - v. Mascheroni, 5 - Tel. 431817
Norvegia - p. Castello, 20 - Tel. 803378
Olanda - v. XX Settembre, 11 - Tel. 870300
Panama - v. Bagutta, 3 - Tel. 705220
Paraguay - c. Venezia, 10 - Tel. 782394
Perù - c. Venezia, 50 - Tel. 706840
Polonia - v. Camperio, 1 - Tel. 878692
Portogallo - v. Pisani, 31 - Tel. 650230
Repubblica **Centro Africana** - Gall. **Unione,** 3 - **Tel.** 803483
Repubblica Costa d'Avorio - v.le Monterosa, 11 - Tel. 490307
Repubblica di San Marino - v. Melegnano, 2 - Tel. 8383
Repubblica Dominicana - v. Zuretti, 23 - Tel. 6884621
S. Marino - v. Chiaramonti, 11 - Tel. 4035620
Senegal - v. delle Asole, 2 - Tel. 879523

Somalia - v. Visc. di Modrone, 21 - Tel. 706326
Spagna - v. Monte Rosa, 3 - Tel. 482337
Stati Uniti d'America - p. Repubblica, 32 - Tel. 652841
Sud Africa - p. de Angeli, 9 - Tel. 4697316
Svezia - v. Broletto, 44 - Tel. 803688
Svizzera e Liechtenstein - v. Palestro, 2 - Tel. 795515
Thailandia - v. Piero della Francesca, 45 - Tel. 314393
Turchia - v. S. Barnaba, 30 - Tel. 573370
Uruguay - p. Diaz, 7 - Tel. 896786
Venezuela - **v. Torriani**, 31 - **Tel. 654136**

TOURIST ORGANIZATIONS

Aero Club Milano - Aeroporto di Bresso - Tel. 924750

Ass. Amici del Po - v. Buonarroti, 28 - Tel. 433403

Ass. Italia Nostra - v. Silvio Pellico, 1 - Tel. 871924

Ass. Lombarda Albergatori - p.za Belgioioso, 1 - Tel. 803341

Ass. Pubblici esercizi - p.za Belgioioso, 1 - Tel. 803241

Ass. Alberghi per la Gioventù - c.so Italia, 10 - Tel. 808781

Ass. Lombarda Uffici Viaggio e Turismo - v. Marconi, 1 - Palazzo del Turismo - Tel. 865096

Azienda Nazionale Autonoma Strade Statali (ANAS) - p.za Sraffa, 11 - Tel. 857.641

Camping Club Lombardo - c.so Italia, 10 - Tel. 808751

Centro Turistico della Tunisia - v. Albricci, 10 - Tel. 863.285

Club Alpino Italiano - v. Silvio Pellico, 6 - Tel. 808421

C.O.N.I. - v. Crivelli, 30 - Tel. 593002

Ente Nazionale Assistenza Lavoratori - ENAL v. Ugo Foscolo, 3 - Tel. 861251

Ente Nazionale Austriaco per il Turismo - v. Dogana, 2 - Tel. 803532

Ente Nazionale Turismo Francese - v. S. Andrea, 5 - Tel. 700268

Ente Provinciale per il Turismo - Uffici Informazioni: palazzo del Turismo - p.za Duomo - Tel. 808813 - Staz. Centrale - Tel. 206.030

Ente Sardo Industrie Turistiche - v. Galvani, 12 - Telefono 680990

Federazione Esperantista - casello di p.ta Venezia - p.le Oberdan, 1

Federazione Italiana Escursionismo - v. Olmetto, 1

Federazione Italiana Sport Invernali - v. Cerva, 30 - Telefono 705167 - v. Quadrio, 11 - Tel. 650940

Federazione Italiana Sci Nautico - v. Zuretti, 102 - Telefono 696233

Istituto Professionale Alberghiero - v. Filippo Tajani, 12 - (Ortica) - Tel. 723889

La Fiera Internazionale di Milano, il massimo mercato campionario d'Italia, che si è affermata quale grande rassegna della produzione mondiale e alla quale partecipano espositori di quasi tutti i principali Paesi del mondo. Si tiene ogni anno dal 14 al 25 aprile.

Palazzo della Permanente - v. Turati, 34.

Rotary Club - v. Cavallotti, 13 - Tel. 709818

SKAL CLUB - C.so Venezia, 11 - Tel. 793635

Touring Club Italiano - c.so Italia, 10 - Tel. 808751

Triennale di Milano - Esposizione internazionale delle Arti decorative e industriali moderne e dell'Architettura moderna che si svolge nel Palazzo dell'Arte al Parco.

Turismo Scolastico del T.C.I. - c.so Italia, 10 - Tel. 803013

Ufficio Informazioni del Comune di Milano - Stazione Metrò - p.za Duomo - Tel. 870545

Ufficio Informazioni Turistiche della Sicilia - c.so Vittorio Emanuele, 37 B (Galleria del Toro) - Tel. 700.028

Ufficio Informazioni Turistiche Valtellina e Valchiavenna - Gall. Vitt. Emanuele, 2 - Tel. 873650

Ufficio Nazionale Spagnolo del Turismo - v. del Don, 5 (ang. v. Disciplini) - Tel. 897.476

Ufficio Nazionale Svizzero del Turismo - p.za Cavour, 4 - Tel. 795602

Ufficio Informazioni delle Ferrovie dello Stato - Stazione Centrale - Tel. 222441

Ufficio Informazioni delle Ferrovie Nord Milano - p.le Cadorna, 14 - Tel. 864051 - 875471

Ufficio Turistico Bulgaro - v. Albricci, 7 - Tel. 866671

Ufficio Turistico Trentino-Dolomiti - v. Dante, 8 - Telefono 807985

Unione Italiana Autonoleggiatori - p.za Aspromonte, 28 - Tel. 278366/203484

GIRI TURISTICI IN AUTOPULLMAN

Per informazioni e prenotazioni rivolgersi agli Uffici Viaggi e Turismo.

Giro di Milano - Tutti i giorni partenza alle ore 9 e alle ore 14,30 da P.za Duomo.

Visita alla città di Monza - dal 1 giugno al 30 settembre - Tutti i giorni feriali partenza alle ore 9 da P.za Castello 1 e alle 9,15 da P.za Duomo.

Visita alla Certosa di Pavia - Tutti i giorni escluso il lunedì dal 1 aprile al 10 ottobre - Festivo dal 1 gennaio al 31 marzo e dall'11 ottobre al 31 dicembre - Partenza alle ore 14,30 da P.za Castello 1.

Gita al Lago di Como - Dal 1 aprile al 30 settembre tutti i giorni - Partenza alle ore 9 da P.za Castello 1.

Giro dei Laghi Lombardi - Dal 1 aprile al 31 ottobre tutti i giorni - Partenza alle ore 9 dalla Stazione Centrale (Galleria delle Carrozze).

CHEMIST'S SHOPS (OPEN DAY AND NIGHT)

ZONA DUOMO:

Alleanza Farmaceutica - v. Correnti, 14 - Tel. 800296
Carlo Erba - p. Duomo, 21 - Tel. 800077
Coop. Farmaceutica - Pass. Duomo, 2 - Tel. 872266
Fontana - p. Fontana, 6
Zambeletti - p. S. Carlo, 1 - Tel. 701526

ZONA GARIBALDI:

Farini - Via Farini, 39 - Tel. 690366
Humanitas - v. F. Filzi, 8 - Tel. 637737
Sanitas - c. Garibaldi. 49 - Tel. 896843
Scevola - v. Fulvio Testi, 74 - Tel. 6425950
Staz. Centrale - Interno Galleria - Tel. 278301

ZONA VENEZIA:

Abruzzi - Abruzzi, 23 - Tel. 278219
Ambreck - Stradivari, 1 - Tel. 209491
Fiore - c. Buenos Aires, 39 - Tel. 221479
Formaggia - c. Buenos Aires, 4 - Tel. 221780
Marinoni - c. Buenos Aires, 55 - Tel. 200513
Nascimbeni - c. Buenos Aires, 70 - tel. 279139

ZONA VITTORIA:

Grischott Ferrarini - p. Cinque Giornate, 6 - Tel. 541471

ZONA VIGENTINA:

Corsico - p. Buozzi, 1 - Tel. 540117
Omero - v.le Omero, 26 - Tel. 537347

ZONA TICINESE:

Giambellino - v. Giambellino, 64 - Tel. 470636
Ticinese - c. S. Gottardo, 1 - Tel. 8480773

ZONA MAGENTA:

Bracco - v. Boccaccio, 26 - Tel. 871645
Oppezzo - v.le Ranzoni, 2 - Tel. 464681

RAILWAYS

MILANO CENTRALE - Informazioni - Tel. 222441
Ferrovie Adriatico Appennino (Società) - foro Bonaparte,
   76 - Tel. 876508
Ferrovie Britanniche - v. Pirelli, 11 - Tel. 667970
Ferrovie Federali Svizzere - p. Cavour, 4 - Tel. 700975
Ferrovie Francesi - v. Meravigli, 12 - Tel. 898447
Ferrovie Federali Austriache - v. S. Paolo, 13 - Tel. 866996
Ferrovie Federali Germaniche - c.so Vitt. Emanuele, 15 -
   Tel. 700182
Ferrovie Jugoslave - p. Diaz, 7 - Tel. 879492
SCALO FARINI - v. Valtellina, 5 - Tel. 691378
MI - CERTOSA - v. Mambretti, 1 - Tel. 302861
MI - CORSICO - Tel. 4471065
MI - GARIBALDI - v. G. Ferrari, 12 - Tel. 662078
MI - GENOVA - p.za Staz. Genova - Tel. 8480382
MI - GRECO - PIRELLI p.za Egeo, 8 - Tel. 2571768
MI - LAMBRATE - P. Bottini - Tel. 293652
MI - ROMANA - c.so Lodi, 51 - Tel. 540183
MI - VITTORIA - v. Umbria, 116 - Tel. 540127
MI - ROGOREDO - v. Toffetti, 20 - Tel. 5399065
MI - SMISTAMENTO - Ortica - Tel. 7388287
MI - S. CRISTOFORO - P. Tirana, 32 - Tel. 4155831
MI - SESTO SAN GIOVANNI - Tel. 241131

FERROVIE NORD

Informazioni: p. Cadorna, 14 - Tel. 875471
MI - NORD - Bullona - P. Della Francesca, 64 - Tel. 341538
MI - NORD - Bovisa - Tel. 370135
MI - NORD - Quarto Oggiaro - Tel. 3551725

METROPOLITANA MILANESE - M.M.
Direzione - v. Vecchio Politecnico, 8 - Tel. 7747
v. Anassagora - Tel. 2576086

GRANDI MAGAZZINI

COIN - S.p.A.

P.za V Giornate
C.so Vercelli
P.le Loreto
Via Rismondo, 8
C.so Garibaldi, 72/1
Via Padova, 200
P.le Cantore, 12

DROP - S.p.A.

Via Conservatorio, 7
V.le Sarca, 223
V.le Brenta
Via Speronari, 8
Via Bligny, 23/A
Via Sarpi, 55/2
Via Soderini
Via Orefici, 2
Via Ariberto, 1
Via Larga, 4
Via Pier Capponi, 1
C.so Ticinese, 53
P.za Loreto, 11
P.za Susa, 1
C.so Buenos Aires, 54

GAMMA D.I. S.p.A.

P.le Lodi
Via Oltrocchi, 11
P.za IV Novembre
P.za Dergano, 9
Via Medeghino, 9/11

LA RINASCENTE UPIM S.p.A.

Via Dante, 5
P.za S. Babila, 5
Via Cuneo, 2
Via Farini, 81
C.so XXII Marzo, 15
Via Masolino da Panicale, 7
Via Spadari, 2
P.le Loreto, 5
P.le Corvetto
C.so S. Gottardo, 29/31
Via Giambellino, 7
P.za Giov. d. Bande Nere
Via A. Traversi, 18
Via Astesani, 37

MAGAZZINI A PREZZO UNICO CON REPARTO ALIMENTARE

MAGAZZINI STANDA S.p.A.

C.so Buenos Ayres, 37
Via P. Sarpi, 33
V.le Montenero, 6
Via Palla/Torino
C.so Vercelli, 8
Via Pattari, 1/3
P.le Susa
P.za Diocleziano, 2/6
L.go Cairoli

V.le Suzzani, 19
Via Palmanova-Cesana
Via Lorenteggio-Redaelli
Via Trau, 3
Via Bordoni, 10
P.za Gambara
Via Uruguay, 6
Via Baroni, 25
Via Mosca, 75/30
Via Betulle, 12
Via Ripamonti, 175
V.le Bligny

SUPERMERCATI ALIMENTARI

SUPERMARKET ITALIANI S.p.A.
V.le Regina Giovanna, 34
V. Domenichino-Monterosa
Via Bergamo, 10
V.le Zara, 123
Via Morgantini, 15
Via Mac Mahon, 128
Via Pezzotti
Via Amoretti, 4/6
Via Forze Armate - Val Devero
Via Losanna, 20/22
P.za Ovidio-Toscolano
Via Feltre - Crescenzago
Via Innominato, 6
V.le Ungheria, 12
Via Cagliero, 14
Via Novara, 90/4
Via Vigliani, 57
Via Lorenteggio, 230
Via Certosa-Armenia
Via Ripamonti, 181
Via Ornato, 28
Via Chiesa Rossa - Neera

S.M.A. SUPERMERCATI S.p.A.
Via Venini, 50
Via Soresina, 1
Via Lomellina, 1
C.so Lodi, 130
Via Padova, 224
L.go Scalabrini, 1
Via Mancini, 4
C.so S. Gottardo, 29/31
Via Astesani, 46
Via M. Ammiano, 14
Via Brocchi, 24
Via Marghera, 5
Via Pacinotti, 14
Via Muratori, 27
Via Canova, 37

STELLA SUPERMARKETS S.I.A.S. - S.p.A.
V.le Abruzzi-D. d'Aosta
Via Monti, 55
Via S. Marcellina-Testi
V.le Famagosta, 16
Via Lorenteggio, 3
P.za Angilberto, 9
Via Medeghino, 11
Via Rismondo, 8/10
Via Coni Zugna ang. C. Colombo

SUPERMERCATI
Via Forze Armate, 44
Via Padova, 111
Via Tolstoi, 61
Via Foppa, 33
Via Strigelli, 8
Via Piccinni, 2
Via Olona, 1/3
Via Inganni, 87
Via Sabotino, 6

SOCIETA' GENERALE SUPERMERCATI S.p.A.
Via Farini, 79/81
V.le Monza, 134
Via Spinoza, 2
P.za Siena
Via Soderini, 48
C.so Lodi-Brenta

SUPERMARKETS UNES
V.le Sabotino, 3
P.za Chiesa D., 2
Via Ripamonti, 110
Via Belisario, 3
Via Val di Sole, 12
Via Varesina, 92

P A M
Via Olona

MINISTERI

Agricoltura e Foreste - v. Juvara, 9 - Tel. 230372 - 292635
Finanze - v. Manin, 27 - Tel. 662605
Lavoro e Previdenza Sociale - v. V. Monti, 51 - Tel. 490182
Sanità - c.so P. Vittoria, 27 - Tel. 701821
Trasporti e Aviazione Civile - v. Turati, 6/8 - Tel. 639354

Monuments, Museums, picture-galleries, libraries, art galleries

Monuments

Duomo - p. Duomo
Visita al tetto del Duomo
   Con ascensore L. 250, a piedi L. 100.
Orario Estivo (1º Aprile-30 Settembre) dalle ore 8 alle 18.
Orario Invernale (1º Ottobre-31 Marzo) dalle ore 8,30 alle 16.
Arco della Pace - p.le Sempione.
Acquario - v.le G. Gadio, 2 - Chiuso lunedì - **Ingresso gratuito.**
Basilica di S. Eustorgio - p.za S. Eustorgio.
Basilica di S. Lorenzo, Colonne Romane - Museo c.so di Porta Ticinese, 29.
Casa di riposo dei Musicisti « G. Verdi » - p.za Buonarroti, 29
Chiesa di S. Gottardo in Corte - v. Pecorari.
Chiesa di S. Maria delle Grazie - p.za S. Maria delle Grazie.
Chiesa di S. Satiro - v. Torino.
Conservatorio di Musica « G. Verdi » - v. Conservatorio, 12.
Galleria Vittorio Emanuele II - p.za Duomo.
Monumento ai Caduti Milanesi nella Guerra 1915-18 - p.za S. Ambrogio.
Planetario - Giardini Pubblici - c.so Venezia, 57 - **Martedì-Giovedì-Sabato** ore 21 - Domenica e festivi infrasettimanali ore 17 e ore 21 - Ingresso L. 200 - Ridotto L. 100 - Chiuso dal 30 Giugno al 1º Ottobre.
Piazza dei Mercanti (Loggia degli Osii, Palazzo della Ragione - Palazzo dei Giureconsulti)
Siloteca Cormio - p.za S. Vittore, 21 - Ingresso gratuito - Chiuso sabato e domenica.
Teatro alla Scala - p.za Scala.
Terraquarium - Passaggio sotterraneo fra le stazioni Duomo-Cordusio della Metropolitana - Aperto nei giorni feriali e festivi - L. 300.
Torre del Parco (m. 109) - Ascensore per la terrazza - belvedere - bar - Biglietto L. 250.

Museums

Cenacolo Vinciano - p.za S. Maria delle Grazie - Ingresso L. 200 nei giorni feriali - L. 100 nei giorni festivi infrasettimanali; gratuito alla domenica - Chiuso lunedì non festivi.

Cimitero Monumentale - p.le Cimitero Monumentale - Orario: 1º Ottobre - 31 Marzo ore 8,30-16,45 - 1º Aprile - 30 Settembre ore 8,30-17,45.

Museo Archeologico - c.so Magenta, 15 - Chiuso martedì - Ingresso gratuito.

Museo d'Arte Antica nel Castello Sforzesco - p.za Castello - Biblioteca Civica - Archivio Storico - Biblioteca d'Arte - Civica raccolta delle Stampe « Achille Bertarelli » - Biblioteca Trivulziana - Medagliere Milanese - Raccolte di antichi strumenti musicali - Ingresso gratuito - Lunedì chiuso.

Museo del Cinema - v. Palestro, 16 - Gratuito - Chiuso sabato e festivi.

Museo della Basilica di S. Ambrogio - p.za S. Ambrogio - Ingresso L. 100.

Museo del Duomo - p.za Duomo, 12 - Chiuso lunedì non festivi - Ingresso gratuito.

Museo del Risorgimento Nazionale - v. Borgonuovo, 23 - Ingresso gratuito - Lunedì chiuso.

Museo delle Cere - Stazione Centrale Ferrovie Stato. (Orario: 8-24) - Ingresso L. 350.

Museo di armi antiche nella Pusterla di S. Ambrogio - p.za S. Ambrogio, 15 - Ingresso L. 200 - Chiuso sabato pomeriggio, domenica e festivi giugno, luglio, agosto.

Museo di Arte e di Etnologia Estremo Orientale - v. Monterosa, 81 - Ingresso gratuito - Chiuso: lunedì, martedì, mercoledì e venerdì.

Museo di Milano (Palazzo Morando) - v. S. Andrea, 6 - Chiuso lunedì - Ingresso gratuito.

Museo Navale Didattico - v. S. Vittore, 21 - Ingresso gratuito - Chiuso lunedì non festivi.

Museo Nazionale della Scienza e della Tecnica « Leonardo da Vinci » - v. S. Vittore, 21 - Ingresso L. 300 - Domenica e giovedì mattino gratuito. Lunedì chiuso.

Museo Poldi Pezzoli - v. Manzoni, 12 - Ingresso L. 300. Giovedì sera L. 350 - Lunedì chiuso.

Museo Teatrale - p.za della Scala - Ingresso L. 250.

Picture-Galleries

Civica Galleria d'Arte Moderna - Villa Comunale - v. Palestro, 16 - Chiuso martedì - Ingresso gratuito.

Galleria d'Arte Sacra dei Contemporanei - v. Giovanni Teruggia, 14 - Tel. 6421420/1.

Pinacoteca Ambrosiana - p.za Pio XI, 2 - Ingresso L. 200 - Aperta nei giorni feriali e festivi.

Pinacoteca di Brera - v. Brera, 28 - Lunedì chiuso. Ingresso: feriali L. 150; festivi infrasett. L. 75; domenica gratuito.

Libraries

Allori - Villa Litta - Tel. 6450897

v. Albenga, 2 - Tel. 406853

v. Cittadini, 34 - Vialba - Tel. 3555087

v. Grugnola, 3 - Villapizzone - Tel. 391978

v. Gulli - Martinetti - Tel. 4036325

v. Odazio, 9 - Lorenteggio - Tel. 4239973

Biblioteca Ambrosiana - p.za Pio XI, 2 - Sabato pomeriggio e domenica chiuso.

Biblioteca Comunale - c. Vittoria, 6 - Tel. 708203

Biblioteca della Società Storica Lombarda - v. Morone, 1 - Chiuso sabato e giorni festivi.

Biblioteca Francescana - p.za S. Angelo, 2 - Sabato pomeriggio chiuso.

Biblioteca Nazionale di Brera - v. Brera, 28 - Domenica chiuso.

Biblioteca Pubblica Rionale Castello Sforzesco - Tel. 870926

Biblioteca Rionale Calvairate - v. Ciceri Visconti, 1 - Tel. 545696

Biblioteca Rionale G. Rosa - v. Montemartini, 6 - Tel. 560020

Biblioteca Succursale Baggio - v. Pistoia, 10 - Tel. 4596044

v. Pogatschnig, 34 - Q.T. 8 - Tel. 390961

Centro Civico - Tel. 264567

Centro Nazionale di Studi Manzoniani - v. Morone, 1 - Chiuso sabato e giorni festivi.

Museo Civico di Storia Naturale - Giardini Pubblici - c.so Venezia, 55 - Chiuso lunedì - Ingresso gratuito.

Museo Manzoniano - Casa del Manzoni - v. Morone, 1 - Chiuso lunedì e giorni festivi - Ingresso gratuito.

Raccolte Storiche del Comune di Milano - v. Borgonuovo, 23 Biblioteca e Archivio: Sabato pom. e domenica chiuso.

Sezione Guastalla - v. P. Andreani, 10 - Tel. 798582

Parco - Zona Montetondo - Tel. 343053

Sezione Venezia ex Casello Daziario - Tel. 279990
Sezione Vigentina - c.so Porta Vigentina, 15 - Tel. 598775
Ufficio Centrale Biblioteche Scolastiche - v. E. Morosini, 11 - Tel. 559045
Ufficio Distribuzione Libri - Tel. 366520

Arts Galleries

Accademia - v. Fiori Chiari, 2 - Tel. 866.989
Angolare - v. Clerici, 13 - Tel. 899188
Annunciata - v. Manzoni, 46 - Tel. 791.102
Apollinaire - v. Brera, 4 - Tel. 862.821
Ars Italica - v. Marconi, 3A - Tel. 876.533
Arte Centro - v. Brera, 11 - Tel. 865.888
Barbaroux - v. S. Spirito, 19 - Tel. 702.925
Barbieri - v. Brera, 7 - Tel. 875.184
Bergamini - c.so Venezia, 16 - Tel. 702.346
Blu - v. Senato, 18 - Tel. 792.404
Bolzani - c.so Matteotti, 20 - Tel. 701.335
Borgogna - v. Borgogna, 7 - Tel. 704.826
Brera - v. Brera, 16 - Tel. 877.219
Cadario - v. Annunciata, 7 - Tel. 662588
Cairola - v. Senato, 45 - Tel. 794.286
Carini - v. Durini, 7 - Tel. 700.270
Celestini - v. S. Andrea, 11 - Tel. 709.009
Ciranna - v. Pisoni G., 2 - Tel. 653393
Cocorocchia - v. Montenapoleone, 18 - Tel. 795.898
Cortina - v. Fatebenefratelli, 15 - Tel. 650.572
De Nieubourg - v. Borgonuovo, 9 - Tel. 804.086
Del Grattacielo - v. Brera, 10 - Tel. 899004
Dell'Ariete - v. S. Andrea, 5 - Tel. 709.944
Dell'Incisione - v. della Spiga, 33 - Tel. 705.993
Del Lauro - v. del Lauro, 8 - Tel. 808.923
Del Levante - v. della Spiga, 1 - Tel. 706.335
Del Milione - v. Bigli, 2 - Tel. 700.909
Del Naviglio - v. Manzoni, 45 - Tel. 661.538
Delle Colonne - c.so Europa, 16 - Tel. 709.927
Delle Ore - v. Fiori Chiari, 18 - Tel. 803.333
Gavioli - v. Durini, 1 - Tel. 700.024
Geri - c.so Venezia, 10/c - Tel. 702939
Gianferrari - v. Gesù, 19 - Tel. 705.250
Globarte - v.le Tunisia, 29 - Tel. 637.181
Il Cannocchiale - v. Brera, 4 - Tel. 867.518
Il Castello - v. Brera, 16 - Tel. 862.913
Il Cigno - v. Manzoni, 7 - Tel. 808.371

Il Discanto - v. Turati, 7 - Tel. 652.557
Il Sestante - v. della Spiga, 3 - Tel. 700.463
Il Vertice - v. Visconti di Modrone, 29 - Tel. 708.613
Jolas - v. Manzoni, 12 - Tel. 791.884
L'Agrifoglio - v. Montenapoleone, 21 - Tel. 709.066
La Nuova Sfera - v. S. Marco, 14 - Tel. 635.209
Levi - v. Montenapoleone, 12 - Tel. 781.707
Lux - v. Formentini, 5 - Tel. 893.350
Manzoni - v. Manzoni, 38 - Tel. 701.117
Milano - v. Spiga, 46 - Tel. 701.700
Moltiplicata Colophon - p.za Cavour, 1 - Tel. 650090
Mondial - v. Brera, 2 - Tel. 807.291
Montenapoleone - v. Montenapoleone, 6/A - Tel. 709.463
Morone - v. Morone, 6 - Tel. 709.994
Pater - v. Borgonuovo, 10 - Tel. 635.091
Sacerdoti - v. S. Andrea, 17 - Tel. 795.151
Sagittario - v. Brera, 2 - Tel. 872.486
Sant'Ambrogio già Gussoni - v. Manzoni, 41 - Tel. 639.984
Schwarz - v. Gesù, 17 - Tel. 780.261
Schubert - v. Cerva, 42 - Tel. 701.626
Sianesi - v. Durini, 25 - Tel. 700.989
Solaria - v. Gesù, 17 - Tel. 702.854
Stendhal - v. Gesù, 5 - Tel. 781.825
Toninelli - v. S. Andrea, 8 - Tel. 792.369
Trans Art - v. Sacchi, 3 - Tel. 899.950
Trentadue - v. Brera, 6 - Tel. 867.629
Vismara - v. Brera, 30 - Tel. 807.980
Vinciana - v. Gesú, 6 - Tel. 791.055

MOTELS

Italmotel - Lainate - Tel. 9370869
Monica Motel - Pregnana Mil. - Tel. 9303969
Motel Agip - S. Donato Mil. - Tel. 512941
Motel EUR - Trezzano s/N - Tel. 4451951
Motel dei Fiori - v. Spezia - Tel. 8436441
Motel Tripoli - Rosate - Tel. 9088893
Motel Tourist - v.le Testi, 300 - Tel. 6437777

TOWN HALL

Assistenza e Sicurezza Sociale - l.go Treves, 1 - Tel. 6236
Civiche Depositerie - v. Meda, 44 - Tel. 8493235
Magazzino Combustibili - v. Messina, 50 - Tel. 381148
Magazzino Laboratorio Economale - v. Friuli, 30 - Tel. 576141

Magazzino Viveri - v. Sansovino, 9 - Tel. 227490
Municipio di Milano - Autoambulanze - Tel. 7733 - Vigili Urbani, Acqua potabile, Fognature - Tel. 7727
Piano Intercom. Milan. Civ. Studi - v. Pecorari, 3 - Tel. 8868
Protocollo Generale - v. Case Rotte, 2 - Tel. 807697
Ripartizione Annona - v. Larga, 12 - Tel. 870721
Ripartizione Aziende Municipalizzate e Partecipazioni Comunali - v. Guastalla, 8 - Tel. 795720
Ragioneria e Cassa Civica - v. S. Pellico, 16 - Tel. 892544
Ripartizione Decentramento - p. Scala, 2 - Tel. 877273
Ripartiz. Demanio e Patrimonio - v. Larga, 12 - Tel. 864160
Ripartizione Economato - v. F. Sforza, 23 - Tel. 708239
Ripartizione Edilizia Popolare - v. Pirelli, 39 - Tel. 637873
Ripartizione Edilizia Privata - v. Pirelli, 39 - Tel. 637376
Ripartizione Educazione - v. Marconi, 2 - Tel. 8868
Ripartizione Igiene e Sanità - lg. Treves, 1 - Tel. 639793
Ripartiz. Imposte di Consumo - v. Larga, 12 - Tel. 806210
Ripartizione Istituzioni Iniziative Culturali e Turismo - v. Sforza, 23 - Tel. 8868
Ripartizione Legale - v. Marino, 7 - Tel. 861608
Ripartizione Personale - p. Scala, 2 - Tel. 892220
Ripartiz. Servizi e Lavori Pubblici - v. Pirelli, 39 - Tel. 6236
Ripartizione Servizio Parchi e Giardini - v. Pirelli, 39 - Tel. 6236
Ripartizione Sport - v. Marconi, 2 - Tel. 8868
Ripart. Trasp. Traffico, Viabil. - v. Beccaria, 19 - Tel. 8868
Ripartizione Tributi - v. Broletto, 7 - v. Rovello, 2 - v. S. Tomaso, 3 - Tel. 8868
Ripart. Urbanist., Piano Regol. - v. Pirelli, 39 - Tel. 666256
Servizi Statistici - v. Larga, 12 - Tel. 804002
Servizio Acqua Potabile - v. Pirelli, 39 - Tel. 652358
Servizio Acqua Potabile - v. Sforza Ascanio, 91 - Tel. 8493989
Servizi Nettezza Urb., Gestione Autoparco - v. P. Leoni, 2 Tel. 589173
S.I.D. - Servizio Immondizie Domestiche - v. Olgettina, 25 - Tel. 2589
Tipografia Comunale - v. Friuli, 30 - Tel. 585477
Uffici Alloggi - v. Romagna, 26 - Tel. 710739
Uffici Autopubbliche - v. Messina, 53 - Tel. 340672
Uffici Oggetti Rinvenuti - v. Arcimboldi ang. v. Unione, 4 - Tel. 870821
Ufficio del Sindaco - p. Scala, 2 - Tel. 8868
Ufficio del Segretario Generale - p. Scala, 2 - Tel. 8868

Ufficio Informazione del Comune di Milano - Stazione metro-
politana - P. Duomo - Tel. 870545
Ufficio Stampa - p. Scala, 2 - Tel. 806510
Uffici: Stato Civile - Mortuario - Anagrafe - Certificati -
Elettorale - Leva - v. Larga, 12 - c.so P. Romana, 2 -
Tel. 8868
Ufficio Tecnico - v. Pirelli, 39 - Tel. 6236

PARKS AND GARDENS

Campo gioco bambini - Parco Nord - Tel. 335921
Campo gioco bambini - Primaticcio - Tel. 4233706
Campo gioco bambini - « Pucci » - p.za Giovanni XXIII -
Tel. 316651

Giardino della Guastalla - v. F. Sforza - v. S. Barnaba
Giardini della Villa Comunale - v. Palestro, 16
Giardino della Rotonda - v. Besana, 12
Giardino Perego - v. dei Giardini
Giardino Porta Venezia - porta Venezia
Parco delle Basiliche - p.za Sant'Eustorgio
Parco di Baggio - v. A. da Baggio
Parco Lambro/Agreste - Tra v. Palmanova e v. Feltre
Parco Ravizza - Tra v. Bocconi e v.le Toscana
Parco Sempione - Castello Sforzesco
Parco Solari - Tra v.le Coni Zugna e v. Solari
Parco Villa Litta - Affori

BOARDING HOUSES

PRIMA CATEGORIA
Duca - pl. Duca d'Aosta, 6 - Tel. 228359
Montenapoleone - largo S. Babila, 5 - Tel. 701632
Villa Victoria - v. Vitruvio, 18 - Tel. 226420

SECONDA CATEGORIA
Ada - v. Sammartini, 15 - Tel. 6883820
Argentario - c. P. Vittoria, 58 - Tel. 794072
Arianna - c. Buenos Aires, 3 - Tel. 206096
Azzurra - c. XXII Marzo, 32A - Tel. 715347
Brescia - v. Magnasco, 14 - Tel. 437084

Cantore - c. Genova, 25 - Tel. 8487565
Carrobbio - v. Medici, 3 - Tel. 899958
Colombo - c. Buenos Aires, 3 - Tel. 225140
Cordusio - v. Gabrio Casati, 1 - Tel. 804349
Del Corso Vitt. Em. - Galleria del Corso, 1 - Tel. 700575
Donizetti - v. Donizetti, 22 - Tel. 792367
Fabrello - v. Sammartini, 15 - Tel. 683716
Fiorella - v. Marghera, 14 - Tel. 4692302
Giar - v. C. Poerio, 32 - Tel. 270279
Ingegnoli - v. Ingegnoli, 20 - Tel. 2892970
Londra - p.za Argentina, 4 - Tel. 228400
Loreto - v. Porpora, 18 - Tel. 225055
Manzoni - v. Senato, 45 - Tel. 791002
Marinella, v. Gambaia, 4 - Tel. 2850724
Marino - v. F. Carcano, 51 - Tel. 463063
Mignon-Loreto - v. Lulli, 6 - Tel. 2361278
Milano - v. Napo Torriani, 17 - Tel. 665428
Oswald - p.za Duomo, 17 - Tel. 802005
Parva Domus - p.za Argentina, 4 - Tel. 273915
Piceno - vl. Piceno, 21 - Tel. 742491
Principe - c.so Buenos Aires, 75 - Tel. 200886
Redy - v. Porpora, 16 - Tel. 203569
Righi - v. Mascheroni, 10 - Tel. 431308
Suisse-France - v. Mengoni, 2 - Tel. 866708
Ray - v. Mascheroni, 8 - Tel. 463126
Vallazze - v. Vallazze, 14 - Tel. 2361104
Villa Gardenia - v. Goldoni, 24 - Tel. 740625
Villa Maria Luisa - v. Tamburini, 8 - Tel. 431297
Villa Mira - v. Sacchini, 19 - Tel. 2041618
Villa Sandra - v. Washington, 34 - Tel. 490571
Washington - v. Washington, 23 - Tel. 495761

TERZA CATEGORIA

Acapulco - vl. Lombardia, 59 - Tel. 235722
Adri - v. Lulli, 18 - Tel. 235692
Adria - v. C. Poerio, 20 - Tel. 273520
Ala - v. Vitruvio, 24 - Tel. 202695
Alba d'Oro - vl. Piave, 5 - Tel. 793880
Al Paradiso - v. Melzo, 21 - Tel. 278930
Ambrosiana - v. Plinio, 22 - Tel. 279670
Amendola - v. Montebianco, 1 - Tel. 495185
Anna - v. Luosi, 43 - Tel. 2361044
Arco - v. Lulli, 4 - Tel. 296973
Aris - v. Canonica, 79 - Tel. 347421

Arlecchino - v. Paganini, 7 - Tel. 278174
Aspromonte - p.za Aspromonte, 14 - Tel. 2363919
Aurora - v. Buenos Aires, 18 - Tel. 278960
Avio - v. Giason del Maino, 5 - Tel. 483228
Barbieri - v. Settala, 3 - Tel. 273093
Bassi - v. Pontaccio, 2 - Tel. 806421
Berengario - v.le Berengario, 1 - Tel. 430881
Binda - v. Menabrea, 25 - Tel. 600977
Blau - c. di Porta Romana, 18 - Tel. 806110
Boscovich - v. Boscovich, 43 - Tel. 221641
Bozzola - Galleria del Corso, 1 - Tel. 795998
Bruna - v. Ghiberti, 26 - Tel. 487073
Capri - v. Mille, 24 - Tel. 713694
Cardinal Ferrari - v. Mercalli, 23 - Tel. 541077
Carmen - v. Donizetti, 3 - Tel. 795150
Catalani - v. Catalani, 4 - Tel. 292860
Cataldi - v. Settala, 46 - Tel. 220093
Cervi - vl. Corsica, 60 - Tel. 715443
Costanza - v. F. Filzi, 30 - Tel. 664685
Crema - v. Piave, 11 - Tel. 780146
Cremona - v. Porpora, 168 - Tel. 235312
Cuba - v. Ricordi, 14 - Tel. 266470
Dassi - v. Pestalozza, 28 - Tel. 2361162
De Albertis - v. De Albertis, 7 - Tel. 7383409
Dei Mille - v. Mille, 62 - Tel. 713682
Dolomiti - v. Stoppani, 34 - Tel. 2041996
Donisi - p. Cincinnato, 1 - Tel. 666450
Edera - c. Buenos Aires, 3 - Tel. 266214
Edy - v. Forze Armate, 8 - Tel. 4035018
Edvige - v. Scarlatti, 20 - Tel. 206781
Europa - v. Benedetto Marcello, 83 - Tel. 276966
Eva - v. Lazzaretto, 17 - Tel. 632898
Ferri - v. Gignous, 17 - Tel. 482957
Filiberti - v. Donizetti, 4 - Tel. 795281
Flavia - v. Bartolozzi, 14 - Tel. 7381896
Focolare Studente - v. Edolo, 18 - Tel. 6882596
Fratini - v. B. Marcello, 65 - Tel. 222468
Gianni - v. F. Carcano, 46 - Tel. 4692859
Giardino - v. dei Missaglia, 14 - Tel. 8433680
Helen - v. Paganini, 8 - Tel. 2042001
Internazionale - v. Dante, 15 - Tel. 873697
Iride - v. Porpora, 170 - Tel. 296695
Ischia - v. F. Lippi, 43 - Tel. 269045
Italia - v. Vitruvio, 44 - Tel. 221896

Jolanda - c. Magenta, 78 - Tel. 463317
Karin - v. Donizetti, 33 - Tel. 795257
Kennedy - v.le Tunisia, 6 - Tel. 200934
La Caravella - v. C. Hajeck, 18 - Tel. 715449
Lanterna - v. Archimede, 121 - Tel. 726919
Leonardo - v. F. Carcano, 37 - Tel. 482284
Lima - c. Buenos Aires, 47 - Tel. 266527
Lippi - v. F. Lippi, 48 - Tel. 2361205
Livingstone - p.za Aspari, 5 - Tel. 7582481
Magic - v. Copernico, 8 - Tel. 683382
Mari - v. Espinasse, 20 - Tel. 364590
Marie Rose - v. B. Marcello, 83 - Tel. 2043126
Marinoni - v. Settala, 56 - Tel. 222366
Marisa - v. Caccianino, 10 - Tel. 233489
Metrò - vl. Monza, 120 - Tel. 2856918
Mini - v. Castel Morrone, 15 - Tel. 733093
Moscova - v. Moscova, 27 - Tel. 665523
Nazionale - v. Vitruvio, 46 - Tel. 224059
Nullo - v. F. Nullo, 37 - Tel. 714991
Oasi Francescana - v. Arzaga, 23 - Tel. 416319
Omodei - v. Soperga, 19 - Tel. 278228
Oriente - v. Porpora, 52 - Tel. 2361298
Ortensia - v. Vallazze, 19 - Tel. 2361234
Paganini - v. Paganini, 6 - Tel. 273890
Panizza - p.za Aspromonte, 22 - Tel. 2361125
Peppino - v. Piatti, 5 - Tel. 806690
Perla - p.za Aspromonte, 7 - Tel. 273025
Piccadilly - v. U. Bassi, 1/A - Tel. 600826
Porpora - v. Porpora, 132 - Tel. 230288
Primavera - v. Archimede, 117 - Tel. 726701
Rapallo - p.za Aspromonte, 18 - Tel. 2361123
Rizi - v. Lulli, 22 - Tel. 2361271
Rosanna - c. Lodi, 7 - Tel. 544558
Rosati - v. Settala, 48 - Tel. 270332
Rovello - v. Rovello, 18 - Tel. 864396
Sabotino - vl. Sabotino, 16 - Tel. 550296
San Tomaso - v. S. Tomaso, 5 - Tel. 8690360
Sara - v. Sacchini, 17 - Tel. 273737
Savino - v. Pontaccio, 2 - Tel. 876635
Sicilia - v. S. Maurilio, 20 - Tel. 865927
Silva - v. G. Silva, 39 - Tel. 468434
Sirtori - v. Sirtori, 26 - Tel. 200870
Sorriso - c. di Porta Vittoria, 51 - Tel. 795686
Tonoli - c. Vercelli, 2 - Tel. 463660

Torino - p.za S. M. Beltrade, 6 - Tel. 808018
Tricolore - p.za Tricolore, 4 - Tel. 799980
Tunisia - v. Tunisia, 6 - Tel. 270623
Ullrich - c. Italia, 6 - Tel. 873177
Venezia - v. Jommelli, 49 - Tel. 2822135
Villa dei Gerani - v. Domenichino, 43 - Tel. 496757
Villa delle Rose - p.le Crivellone, 12/14 - Tel. 483048
Villa Giovanna - v. Washington, 42 - Tel. 463951

DAY-CLINICS

Poliamb. Buenos Aires - c. Buenos Aires, 18 - Tel. 278485
Poliamb. della Gamboloita - c. Lodi, 107 - Tel. 564108
Poliambulanza di Greco - p. Morbegno, 3 - Tel. 287151
Poliamb. di Porta Venezia - p. Oberdan, 10 - Tel. 221777
Poliambulanza Farini - v. Farini, 55 - Tel. 690694
Pol. La Torretta - v. Fra Cristoforo, 2 - Tel. 8435425
Poliambulanza Magenta - p. Wagner, 2 - Tel. 431532
Poliambulanza Padova - v. Padova, 90 - Tel. 280352
Poliambulanza Ronzoni - v. Ronzoni, 1 - Tel. 8488751

POSTAL AND TELEGRAPH SERVICES

Cassa Provinciale - v. Cordusio, 4 - Tel. 875452
Centrale Telex - p.za Affari, 2 - Tel. 871444
Conti Correnti - v. Tazzoli, 2 - Tel. 669586
Corrispondenze - v. F. Aporti, 8/10 - Tel. 265966
Corrispondenze pacchi Centro - v. Cordusio, 4 - Tel. 807595
Deposito Carte Valori - v. S. Maria Segreta, 3 - Tel. 802516
Direz. Prov. P.T. - v. Cordusio, 4 - 1º Reparto Ispezione -
   v. Tazzoli, 2 - Tel. 669787 - 2º Reparto: Tel. 806941 - 3º
   Reparto: Tel. 802361 - 4º Reparto: Tel. 802364 - 5º Reparto
   Ragioneria: Tel. 803824
Economato Provinciale - v. Tazzoli, 2 - Segr. - Tel. 669990
Posta Pneumatica Urbana - v. Cordusio, 4 - Tel. 893776
Sala Stampa Est. in Italia - v. S. M. Segreta, 3 - Tel. 802066
Sala Stampa Italiana - v. S. Maria Segreta, 3 - Tel. 865082
Settore Centro - v. F. Aporti, 8 - Tel. 273923
Settore Est - Aporti - v. Aporti, 8 - Tel. 203330
Settore Est - Lambrate - v. Aporti, 8 - Tel. 273823
Settore Sud - v. Gargano, 9 - Tel. 5399187
Settore Ovest - v. Massarenti, 22 - Tel. 405712
Settore Nord - v.le Zara, 129 - Tel. 6881664
Ufficio Telegrafico Principale - v. Cordusio, 4 - Tel. 802465

Milano Succ.le 1 - v. Cogne, 14 - Tel. 3555035
Milano Succ.le 2 - p. Liberty, 4 - Tel. 799055
Milano Succ.le 3 - v. Oglio, 7 - Tel. 564655
Milano Succ.le 4 - v. Sebast. del Piombo, 13 - Tel. 4693990
Milano Succ.le 6 - v. P. Lomazzo, 25 - Tel. 339328
Milano Succ.le 7 - v. Vigevano, 32 - Tel. 833388
Milano Succ.le 8 - v. Motta, 5 - Tel. 495176
Milano Succ.le 9 - v.le Sabotino, 21/a - Tel. 542709
Milano Succ.le 10 - c.so B. Aires, 12 - Tel. 279313
Milano Succ.le 11 - v. Zanardelli, 1 - Tel. 790579
Milano Succ.le 12 - v. Sambuco, 15 - Tel. 8397005
Milano Succ.le 14 - v. Pecchio, 1 - Tel. 222843
Milano Succ.le 15 - v. Vigna, 6 - Tel. 862504
Milano Succ.le 16 - v. S. Sofia, 8 - Tel. 803991
Milano Succ.le 17 - v. Pier Marini, 1 - Tel. 339329
Milano Succ.le 18 - v. R. Sanzio - Tel. 430028
Milano Succ.le 19 - v. Cardano, 8 - Tel. 653493
Milano Succ.le 20 - Bastioni Volta, 7 - Tel. 667291
Milano Succ.le 21 - v. Urbano III, 2 - Tel. 872787
Milano Succ.le 22 - v. Porro Lambertenghi, 23 - **Tel. 680538**
Milano Succ.le 23 - v. S. Simpliciano, 5 - Tel. 804601
Milano Succ.le 24 - c. Venezia (ang. v. Salvini) - **Tel. 700324**
Milano Succ.le 25 - c. di Porta Vittoria, 18 - Tel. 794477
Milano Succ.le 26 - v. Moscova, 13 - Tel. 664610
Milano Succ.le 28 - v. Leopardi, 26 - Tel. 862503
Milano Succ.le 29 - v. Grigna, 9 - Tel. 390531

Milano Succ.le 30 - v. Ponti, 31 - Tel. 471492
Milano Succ.le 32 - v. Mazzini, 15 - Tel. 808794
Milano Succ.le 34 - v. Mantova, 5 - Tel. 585573
Milano Succ.le 35 - v. Montevideo, 25 - Tel. 462722
Milano Succ.le 36 - v. Illirico, 11 - Tel. 730617
Milano Succ.le 38 - v. S. Galdino, 4 - Tel. 341536
Milano Succ.le 39 - v. Belinzaghi (v. Menabrea) - T. 606703
Milano Succ.le 40 - v. M. Macchi, 9 - Tel. 203189
Milano Succ.le 41 - v. Boito, 3 - Tel. 804332
Milano Succ.le 42 - v. Monte Nero, 17 - Tel. 585590
Milano Succ.le 43 - v. Ariberto, 3 - Tel. 8394994
Milano Succ.le 44 - v. Battistotti Sassi, 14 - Tel. 7385386
Milano Succ.le 45 - v. Venini, 16 - Tel. 2853749
Milano Succ.le 46 - v. Pomponazzi, 6/5 - Tel. 8493236
Milano Succ.le 47 - v. Monte S. Genesio - Tel. 683735
Milano Succ.le 48 - v. Rimembr. di Lambrate, 7 - T. 296769

Milano Succ.le 49 - v. Carnevali, 113 - Tel. 370330
Milano Succ.le 50 - v. Privata Adelchi, 2 - Tel. 230776
Milano Succ.le 51 - v. Arquà, 14 - Tel. 2822138
Milano Succ.le 52 - v. Pianell (vl. F. Testi) - Tel. 6425960
Milano Succ.le 53 - v. Ripamonti, 110 - Tel. 5399019
Milano Succ.le 54 - v. Bronzino, 7 - Tel. 203195
Milano Succ.le 55 - p. Napoli, 38 - Tel. 471102
Milano Succ.le 56 - v.le Cassiodoro, 4 - Tel. 483680
Milano Succ.le 57 - p. Cavour, 2 - Tel. 794628
Milano Succ.le 58 - v.le Zara, 131 - Tel. 600564
Milano Succ.le 59 - v. Altamura, 1 - Tel. 4080108
Milano Succ.le 60 - p. Tirana, 12 - Tel. 4155854
Milano Succ.le 61 - v. Carabelli, 7 - Tel. 584667
Milano Succ.le 62 - v. Mecenate, 26/2 - Tel. 5061289
Milano Succ.le 63 - v.le Castelmorrone, 2/bis - Tel. 7389590
Milano Succ.le 64 - v. G. Sand, 2 (Affori) - Tel. 6450942
Milano Succ.le 65 - v. Cabella, 6 (Baggio) - Tel. 4590870
Milano Succ.le 66 - v. Mondovì, 2 - Tel. 2569188
Milano Succ.le 67 - v.le Monza (vl. Teocrito) - Tel. 2573404
Milano Succ.le 68 - v. Varesina, 205 - Tel. 302904
Milano Succ.le 69 - v. P. Rotta, 20 (Niguarda) - Tel. 6421569
Milano Succ.le 70 - v. Rogoredo, 1 (Rogoredo) - Tel. 510108
Milano Succ.le 71 - v. Cascina Barocco - Tel. 4592792
Milano Succ.le 72 - v. Comune Antico, 5 - Tel. 6882305
Milano Succ.le 73 - v. Novara, 159 - Tel. 4520430
Milano Succ.le 74 - v.le Ungheria, 4 - Tel. 504038
Milano Succ.le 75 - v. S. Bernardo, 37 - Tel. 592000
Milano Succ.le 76 - v. Teano, 21 - Tel. 6464455
Milano Succ.le 77 - v. S. Gimignano, 10 - Tel. 4152913
Milano Succ.le 78 - v. Ponale, 6 - Tel. 6429418
Milano Succ.le 79 - v. Baroni, 11 - Tel. 8263541
Milano Succ.le 80 - v. Appennini, 21
Milano Succ.le 81 - v. Santa Teresa, 12 - Tel. 8493452

TARIFFE POSTALI

Cartoline e biglietti da visita con la sola firma o con non
più di 5 parole di convenevoli L. 25 per l'Italia e L. 20 per
le altre Nazioni.
Cartoline illustrate per corrispondenza epistolare L. 40 per
l'Italia, L. 55 per le altre Nazioni.

Lettere per i primi 20 grammi: L. 50 per l'Italia, la Francia, il Principato di Monaco, la Germania, il Belgio, il Lussemburgo ed i Paesi Bassi; L. 90 per le altre Nazioni.

Espresso: L. 150 più affrancatura ordinaria per l'Italia; L. 180 più l'affrancatura ordinaria per le altre Nazioni.

PREFECTURE

Prefettura Milano - c. Monforte, 31 - Centralino - Tel. 791241
Ufficio elettorale - Tel. 792341 — Ufficio dell'Addetto Stampa Tel. 701024 — Ufficio Capo Zona Telecomunicaz. - Telefono 781697 — Ufficio Pubbl. Sicurezza - Tel. 791241 — Ufficio Assistenza Tel. 708800

FIRST AID

COORDINAMENTO CHIAMATE URGENTI
Centralino Comunale - v. Beccaria, 19 - Tel. 7733
Croce Azzurra Caval. S. Giorgio - v. Pavoni, 5 - Tel. 679905
Croce Bianca - v. Vettabbia (v. Calatafimi) - Tel. 8471451 - v. Arsia, 7 - Tel. 3555030
Croce Italia - v. Terruggia, 24 - Tel. 6422148 - 6428549
Croce Rosa Celeste - Trasporto bambini - v. Castelvetro, 32 Tel. 389845
Croce Rosa Celeste - v. Viganò, 8 - Tel. 652813
v. Forze Armate, 387 - Tel. 4590170
Croce Rossa Italiana - Socc. Medico Urgente - via Pucci, 7 Tel. 339555
Croce Verde Sempione - p.za Santorre di Santarosa, 10 - Tel. 305468
Croce Verde - v. S. Vincenzo, 25 - Tel. 8390035

Croce Verde Baggio - v. F. Armate, 387 - Tel. 4590170
Croce Viola - v. Guerzoni, 42 - Tel. 603874
Croce d'Oro - via Marochetti, 7 - Tel. 534000

EMERGENCY ADDRESSES

Nucleo Radio Mobile - Tel. 4695140
Nucleo Radio Mobile - v. Monti, 58 - Tel. 4692565-570-890
Nucleo Investigativo - v. Moscova, 19 - Tel. 638258-70
Nucleo Polizia Giudiziaria - v. Freguglia, 1 - Tel. 79405
Auto recuperate - Tel. 4695097

STAZIONI C.C.

Affori - v. Cialdini, 131 - Tel. 6450041
Baggio - v. Montecatini, 14 - Tel. 4229557
Cagnola - v. Tolentino, 1 - Tel. 381531
Città Studi - v. Fiamma, 6 - Tel. 711228
Corsico - Bosso, 7 - Tel. 4471022
Crescenzago - v. Padova, 257 - Tel. 2560080
Duomo - v. Valpetrosa, 2 - Tel. 866183-807031-875191
Garibaldi - v. Copernico, 32 - Tel. 678156
Genova - v. Egadi, 11 - Tel. 431341
Gorla - Precotto - v. P. Finzi, 10 - Tel. 2571165
Gratosoglio - v. Gratosoglio, 63 - Tel. 8260386
Greco - v. Finzi, 10 - Tel. 2576673
Lambrate - v. Bertolazzi, 10 - Tel: 296120
Linate - 719507
Magenta - v. Berengario, 16 - Tel. 435403
Monforte - v. Fiamma, 6 - Tel. 723841-573800
Moscova - v. Moscova, 19 - Tel. 665758
Musocco - v. Mambretti, 27 - Tel. 3570513
Niguarda - v. Grivola, 10 - Tel. 6423412
Novate Milanese - 3541442
Quinto Romano - v. Caldera, 150 - Tel. 4520440
Romana - v. Freguglia, 1 - Tel. 790683
San Cristoforo - v. Montecatini, 14 - Tel. 479430
San Donato Milanese - v. Ospedaletto, 1 - Tel. 5272870
Scalo Centrale - Staz. Centrale - Tel. 665358/9
Sempione - v. Tolentino, 1 - Tel. 381527
Sesto San Giovanni - 2470039
Ticinese - v. Gentilino, 15 - Tel. 8394319
Venezia - v. Copernico, 32 - Tel. 678157
Vigentino - v. Ripamonti, 187 - Tel. 531580
Vittoria - v. Fiamma, 6 - Tel. 712513

QUESTURA CENTRALE

SOCCORSO PUBBLICO - Tel. 113
VOLANTE - v. Fatebenefratelli, 11 - Tel. 6226
Ufficio Notturna - Tel. 652130
Informazioni Passaporto - Tel. 653222-667006
Caserma Garibaldi - P.za S. Ambrogio, 5 - Tel. 8690147
POLIZIA FEMMINILE - Tel. 6226/561/578/478

POLIZIA STRADALE

p.za Prealpi, 1 - Tel. 321641
Autocentro di Polizia - v. Regolo, 33 - Tel. 5060824
Gruppo Polizia Ferroviaria - v. Soperga, 14 - Tel. 270813
Commissariato di P.S. di Frontiera - Aeroporto di Linate - Tel. 716841
Servizio Informazioni dello stato delle strade - Tel. 323447

POLICE-STATIONS

01 - Centro - p.zza S. Sepolcro, 9 - Tel. 862551
 1 - Città Studi - via Cadamosto, 4 - Tel. 278725
 2 - Cenisio - via Chianciano, 6 - Tel. 6453014
 3 - Garibaldi - via Schiaparelli, 8 - Tel. 694067
 4 - Genova - v.le Papiniano, 60 - Tel. 833242
 5 - Greco-Turro - via Delle Leghe, 11 - Tel. 2899647
 6 - Lambrate - via Clericetti, 42 - Tel. 296010
 7 - Magenta - via Spinola ang. Berengario - Tel. 496234
 8 - Monforte - via Poma, 8 - Tel. 719476
 9 - Musocco - via Pantelleria, 7 - Tel. 390364
10 - San Siro - via Novara, 199 - Tel. 4520241
11 - Scalo Romana - via Benaco, 1 - Tel. 560340
12 - Sempione - via Quadrio, 28 - Tel. 664185
13 - Ticinese - via Tabacchi, 6 - Tel. 830240
14 - Venezia - via Boscovich, 42 - Tel. 270025
15 - Vittoria - via Poma, 8 - Tel. 733322
        Sesto San Giovanni - v. B. Croce, 28 - Tel. 2477267

VIGILI DEL FUOCO

v. Messina, 39 - Tel. 22222 - v. Ansperto da Biassono, 4 - Tel. 866178 - pl. Cuoco (ang. v. Carabelli) - Tel. 5460260 - v. Sardegna, 8 - Tel. 430983 - v. Benedetto Marcello, 31 - Tel. 200752 - v. Darwin, 5 - Tel. 8481462 - v.le E. Forlanini (Aeroporto Forlanini) - Tel. 717045

RESTAURANTS

« CAVALLINO » - Dir. Gianni Ronchetti - v. Messina, 8 - Tel. 381367

LA TANA DEL LUPO - Specialità montanare - v.le Vitt. Veneto, 30 - Tel. 639006

OSTERIA DEL VECCHIO CANNETO - v. Solferino, 56 - Tel. 638498 - L'Oste Barracca e le sue specialità di pesce all'abruzzese

POULIREU (Tipico Milanese) - v. Ripamonti, 337 - Tel. 530954

TAVERNA DEL GRAN SASSO - pl. pr. Clotilde. 10 - Tel. 637578

AA - Ai 2 mafiosi - v. Savona, 86 (p.za Napoli) - Tel. 4233615

A Piedigrotta - v. Cesare da Sesto, 5 - Tel. 850642

Abetone - Foro Bonaparte (ang. v. Q. Sella) - Tel. 861406

Agape degli Artisti - v. Sapeto, 1 - Tel. 8488004

Ai Sabbioni - vl. d'Annunzio, 9 - Tel. 8390052

Al Baitone - v. Teodorico, 26 - Tel. 390723

Al Barroccio - c. XXII Marzo, 40 - Tel. 733524

Al Bolognese da Gabriello - v. Merlo, 1 - Tel. 798324

Al Borgia - pl. F.lli Zavattari, 4 - Tel. 468800

Al Buon Convento - c. Italia, 26 - Tel. 890623

Al Cancello - v. Bligny, 60 - Tel. 595588

Al Capriccio - v. Bezzecca, 10 - Tel. 585460

Al Castello - p. del Castello, 2 - Tel. 873814

Al Ceppo da Attilio - v. Soresina, 2 - Tel. 439244

Al Chico - v. Sirtori, 24 - Tel. 266883

Al Ciovassino Ristorante - v. Ciovassino, 5 - Tel. 893868

Ai Colli Toscani - v. Stampa, 8 - **Tel.** 890930

Al Dollaro - v. P. da Cannobio, 11 - Tel. 804138

Al Farwest - vl. Certosa, 106 - Tel. 390422

Al Forchettone - v. Monte Rosa, 20 - Tel. 464839

Al Ghiottone - v. Correnti, 26 - Tel. 873013

Al Girarrosto - c. Venezia, 31 - Tel. 705975

Al Girasole - v. U. Bassi, 22 - **Tel.** 603876

Al Golfo di Napoli - v. Crispi, 7 - **Tel.** 650188

Al Grappolo - p. Napoli, 9 - Tel. 4229568

Al Grattacielo - v. V. Pisani, 6 - Tel. 632330

Al Griso - v. F. Filzi, 12 - **Tel.** 664963

Al Matarel - v. Solera Mantegazza, 2 - Tel. 654204

Al Mercante - p.za Mercanti, 17 - Tel. 892198

Al Muleto - v. XXII Marzo, 57 - Tel. 726814

Al Pirata - c. Lodi, 93 - Tel. 560089
Al Ponte Vecchio - p. Mentana, 10 - Tel. 860036
Al Porto - pl. Cantore - Tel. 8471481
Al Sasso di Dante - v. Tavazzano, 6 - Tel. 366452
Al Senato - v. Senato, 43 - Tel. 702802
Al Vecchio Convento - v. Ricordi, 8 - Tel. 206987
Al Vecchio Passeggero - v. Gherardini, 1 - Tel. 312461
Al Vicerè - v. Fogazzaro, 14 - Tel. 581158
Alba d'Oro - v. G.B. Morgagni, 40 - Tel. 225259
Albergo Bel-Sit - vl. Certosa, 85 - Tel. 391413
Alduccio - v. Maddalena, 1 - Tel. 807945
Alfio Cavour - v. Senato, 31 - Tel. 700633
Alla Bella Pisana - v. Sottocorno, 17 - Tel. 708376
Alla Collina Pistoiese - v. Amedei, 1 - Tel. 806613
Alla Mantovana, di Serafini C. - v. Volta, 3 - Tel. 664108
All'Ostricaro (Casello Autostr. Sesto S. Giov.) - Tel. 9286350
Alle Asse - v. Marcona, 6 - Tel. 795359
Alle Cascine - v. Turati, 7 - Tel. 635879
Allo Scudo - v. Mazzini, 7 - Tel. 892761
Altopascio - v. Fara, 17 - Tel. 666452
American Hotel - v. Finocchiaro Aprile, 2 - Tel. 667413
Angelo (dell') - v. Larga, 4 - Tel. 806846
Antica Brasera Meneghina - v. Circo, 10 - Tel. 808108
Antille - v. Delfico, 39 - Tel. 389411
Aquileja - pl. Aquileja, 12 - Tel. 436915
Arc En Ciel - v. Del Mare, 49 - Tel. 8431346
Ardo & Liria - vl. Montesanto, 2 - Tel. 653846
Arlecchino - v. Pier Luigi da Palestrina, 9 - Tel. 220631
Astoria - vl. Murillo, 9 - Tel. 406851
Bagutta - v. Bagutta, 14 - Tel. 702767
Balkan - c.so Sempione, 76 - Tel. 317880
Bar al Caminetto - v. dal Re, 38 - Tel. 366047
Bar Costanza - v. Filzi, 30 - Tel. 632105
Bar Derna - v. Derna, 13 - Tel. 2893572
Bar Due Torri - p. Napoli, 30/2 - Tel. 479774
Bar Franco - v. Monte Cenisio, 8 - Tel. 384511
Bar Laghi - pl. ai Laghi, 3 - Tel. 302952
Bar Leonardo da Vinci, p.za L. Da Vinci, 10 - Tel. 292553
Bar Rist. al 51 - v. Monza, 51 - Tel. 286117
Bar Ristorante Istria - vl. Testi, 5 - Tel. 674912
Bar Rist. la Baracca, Di Fabio - c.so Lodi, 4 - Tel. 588577
Bar Rist. The Kilt - v. Paolo da Cannobio, 1 - Tel. 875396
Bassi I. - v. Pomponazzi, 9 - Tel. 8493868

Bavaria - v. Plinio, 63 - Tel. 200960
Bell'Aria - v. Ludovico il Moro, 119 - Tel. 470524
Belloni G. - v. Torino, 50 - Tel. 807650
Bergna A. - v. dell'Orso, 12 - Tel. 893581
Biffi - gall. Vitt. Eman. II - Tel. 806541
Birreria Porta Renza - v. Tunisia, 1 - Tel. 276473
Boccaccio - p. Virgilio, 3 - Tel. 802631
Boeucc - p. Belgioioso, 2 - Tel. 790224
Bollani A. - v. Ripamonti, 204 - Tel. 564519
Bolognese la Pergola - v. Valenza, 13 - Tel. 8480877
Botte d'Oro - v. Casati, 5 - Tel. 278292
Brambillone - v. P. Mantegazza, 33 - Tel. 390210
Brera - v. Pontaccio, 9 - Tel. 893083
Ca' Bianca - v. Lodovico il Moro, 117 - Tel. 479264
Ca' D'Oro - v. Perasto, 2/a - Tel. 683095
Calatti - Trattoria della Pesa - v. Pasubio, 10 - Tel. 665741
Casa Mia - v.. Faruffini, 15 - Tel. 496587
Cascina Corba - v. Gigli, 14 - Tel. 427627
Cavallini - v. Macchi, 2 - Tel. 200297
Cavallino - Dir. G. Ronchetti - v. Messina, 8 - Tel. 381367
Chateau d'Avignon - v. S. Maurilio, 20 - Tel. 870255
Chiavacci A. - p. Oberdan, 2/a - Tel. 279528
Ciardi S. - v. S. Raffaele, 6 - Tel. 800411
Cinese « Da Ming » - v. Giusti, 41 - Tel. 314119
Cinese « La Pagoda » - v. Filzi, 2 - Tel. 654700
Cirano - v. Manfredini, 12 - Tel. 381847
Circolo « Milan Noeuva » - v. Verri, 8 - Tel. 792730
Cocchi S. « da Celesta » - v. Losanna, 11 - Tel. 342996
Collina Pistoiese - v. Amedei, 1 - Tel. 806613
Conchiglia - v. Messina, 4 - Tel. 389869
Conty Grill - v. Romagnosi, 2 - Tel. 807641
Coppa P. - v. Marghera, 2 - Tel. 490597
Corbelli E. - vl. Certosa, 298 - Tel. 304680
Cortesi - v. Orefici, 26 - Tel. 892198
Cosmello - v. G.B. Grassi, 67 - Tel. 3555193
Covino G. - v. Manara, 13 - Tel. 794012
Crispi Ristorante da Flaminio - c.so Venezia, 3 - Tel. 782010
Cucina Toscana - vl. Bligny, 42 - Tel. 540093
Da Angelo - vl. Umbria, 60 - Tel. 584668
Da Berti - v. Algarotti, 20 - Tel. 691696
Da Bice - v. Borgospesso, 12 - Tel. 702572
Da Bruno - v. Gonzaga, 6 - Tel. 804364
Da Carletto e Fiorella - v. S. Agnese, 16 - Tel. 896185

Da Cesare - v. Fiamma, 19 - Tel. 747142
Da Emilio - v. dei Bossi, 5 - Tel. 871068
Da Eva e Bruno - v. G. Albricci, 3 - Tel. 806356
Da Ezio - v. Ariberto, 1 - Tel. 851461
Da Furio - v. G. Negri, 4 - Tel. 870602
Da Gigi il Cacciatore - v. Procaccini, 54 - Tel. 389965
Da Gino Riviera Toscana - v. Sciesa, 18 - Tel. 553782
Da Lino - v. F. Casati, 19 - Tel. 273383
Da Loretto - v. G. Uberti, 5 - Tel. 733047
Da Marino, al Conte Ugolino - p.za Beccaria, 6 - Tel. **876134**
Danilo - v. S. F. d'Assisi, 2 - Tel. 554053
Dante « Da Primo » - v. Porlezza, 2 - Tel. 897386
Da Pietro - v. Settala, 2 - Tel. 278905
Da Renato - v. L. Palazzi, 19 - Tel. 265982
Da Renato - v. Pontaccio, 3 - Tel. 892927
Da Renzo - v. Teodosio, 104 - Tel. 286261
Da Roberto - Foro Buonaparte, 8 - Tel. 892174
Da Rolando, Alle Colline Fior. - v. Statuto, 16 - Tel. 662219
Da Settimo - v. Giambellino, 67 - Tel. 470540
Da Terzilio - v. Gluck, 10 - Tel. 606709
Davos - v. Melloni, 18 - Tel. 7388274
Dei Magnani - v. Agnello, 19 - Tel. 800591
De Liso D. - v. Novara, 101 - Tel. 4080059
De Rosa - v. Colonnetta, 5 - Tel. 794173
De Vincenzo G. - v. Maloja, 10 - Tel. 691937
Don Abbondio - v. Cavezzali, 11 - Tel. 2827484
Don Chisciotte - v. Palmanova, 153 - Tel. 2564098
Don Lisander - v. Manzoni, 12/a - Tel. 790130
El Bramantin - v. Bramante, 1 - Tel. 381704
Eliseo - p. S. Stefano, 5 - Tel. 861321
El Ronchett - v. Lodovico il Moro, 167/169 - Tel. 4228354
Er Principe - v. Principe Eugenio, 15 - Tel. 344040
Fallabrino L. - v. Padova, 133 - Tel. 2826120
Ferrario - p. del Duomo, 17 - Tel. 806191
Fiorentina - v. Sciesa, 3 - Tel. 542912
Fiorenza - vl. Certosa, 223 - Tel. 305226
Fiori Oscuri American Bar - v. Fiori Oscuri, 3 - Tel. 890181
Firenze « Da Eugenio » - v. Foscolo, 1 Tel. 870281
Firenze « Da Luciano » - v. Foscolo, 1 - Tel. 866818
Fontana L. - v. Ornato, 8 - Tel. 6422003
Fontanelli B - v. Palazzi, 5 - Tel. **270626**
Fontanelli I. - v. Marino, 7- Tel. 800197

Fontanelli - p. del Liberty, 8 - Tel. 798631
Fortuna - v. Teodosio, 6 - Tel. 2361172
Foyer - v. Verdi, 6 - Tel. 862210
Fra Diavolo - v. della Palla, 3 - Tel. 875040
Furio Rist. - v. Berengario, 1 - Tel. 495677
Galbiati - v. Scoglio di Quarto, 3 - Tel. 8472454
Gallo Nero - p. Corvetto, 3 - Tel. 5392056
Gallo Rosso - v. Dandolo, 2 - Tel. 795034
Gamba de Legn (El) - v. Elba, 30 - Tel. 463091
Gambero Rosso - p. del Castello, 1 - Tel. 804495
Gamma - v. Valvassori Peroni, 85 - Tel. 235366
Gargani E. - c. Genova, 25 - Tel. 857315
Gaudio I. - c. Lodi, 130 - Tel. 537265
Giacobbe G. - v. Lecco, 3 - Tel. 225076
Giannina - p.za Diocleziano - Tel. 335802
Giannino E.R.E.A. - v. Sciesa, 8 - Tel. 542765
Giggi Fazi - Hostaria Romana - v. Poerio, 2/a - Tel. 747097
Giglio Rosso - da Ermo - p. Luigi di Savoia, 2 - Tel. 266428
Giglio Rosso - v. Rovello, 10 - Tel. 874292
Giongrandi F. - v. Vigevano, 45 - Tel. 8480148
Giordano - c. Genova, 3 - Tel. 8480824
Gonzales - v. Filzi, 25 - Tel. 653216
Gourmet - v. Torino, 2 - Tel. 897571
Gran Maracanà - vl. Abruzzi, 19 - Tel. 270580
Gran San Bernardo - v. Borgese, 14 - Tel. 389000
Grattacielo di Milano - v. F. Casati, 45 - Tel. 632491
Harry's Bar - Gall. di v. Manzoni, 40 - Tel. 700331
Holiday House - v. Pier Luigi Palestrina, 2 - Tel. 208808
Il Balordo - c. Sempione, 12 - Tel. 389666
Il Brigante - v. S. Tecla, 3 - Tel. 808900 - 862715
Ii Giaguaro - vl. Famagosta, 31 - Tel. 819417
Il Morso - v. Ripamonti, 166 - Tel. 5397871
Il Paiolo - v. Traiano, 62 - Tel. 390467
Il Paladino - vl. Tunisia, 6 - Tel. 278612
Il Posto - c.so Sempione ang. v. Prina - Tel. 312760
Il Quadrante - v. Mengoni, 4 - Tel. 807367
Italia - v. Pozzone, 1 - Tel. 874298
La Baia - v. Cellini, 3 - Tel. 704269
La Barcarola - v. Volta, 9 - Tel. 667265
La Buca - v. Torriani, 28 - Tel. 206646
La Bussola - v. Castaldi, 4 - Tel. 635767
La Cantinetta - v. Ripamonti, 19 - Tel. 580817
La Capanna Fiorentina - v. Arimondi, 11 - Tel. 322138

La Collina - v. Napo Torriani, 25 - Tel. 669476
La Colonnina - c. Italia, 16 - Tel. 873725
« La Festa » - vl. Lombardia, 68 - Tel. 2893430
La Forca - p. Diaz, 5 - Tel. 860598
La Fortuna - v. Foppa, 40 - Tel. 425774
La Frasca - v. Foldi, 1 - Tel. 573404
La Grotta - v. Bergamini, 13 - Tel. 862917
La Garfagnana - p. Cincinnato, 4 - Tel. 273832
La Lanterna Fiorentina - v. f.lli Bronzetti, 8 - Tel. 740400
La Maggiolina - v. Torelli Viollier, 26/A - Tel. 690791
La Nos - v. Amedei, 2 - Tel. 898759
La Pampa - v. Conca del Naviglio, 37 - Tel. 8473524
La Pantera - v. Festa del Perdono, 12 - Tel. 897374
La Pianta - vl. Affori, 1 - Tel. 6450034
L'Aratro - v. Marocco, 12 - Tel. 2850126
La Racchetta - c.so Europa - Tel. 780860
L'Aretino - p. U. Giordano, 4 - Tel. 790827
L'Assassino - v. Amedei, 8 - Tel. 896144
La Sirenella - v. Lorenteggio, 157 - Tel. 421316
La Sirenetta - v. Carabelli, 7/9 - Tel. 5461890
La Stalla Romana - vl. Vigliani, 55 - Tel. 4695586
La Tampa - v. Laghetto, 3 - Tel. 793300
La Tana del Lupo - v.le Vitt. Veneto, 30 - Tel. 639006
La Tegola - vl. Cassiodoro, 5 - Tel. 436966 - 463713
La Villetta - v. Bezzi, 86 - Tel. 435293
La Villetta - v. Cremosano, 41 - Tel. 390646
La Villetta - vl. Zara, 87 - Tel. 671981
Lazy Jack - v. Crocefisso, 27 - Tel. 899333
Le Cinque Terre - v. Appiani, 9 - Tel. 651650
Londonio «Da Nello » - v. Londonio, 22 - Tel. 399009
L'Ortolano - Nuovo Mercato Ortofrutticolo - v. Lombroso,
    54 - Tel. 542508
Lo Scrigno - c.so Lodi, 70 - Tel. 563081
Lo Spadaccino - v. Luini, 7 - Tel. 872148
Lotito - p. Belfanti, 6 - Tel. 8486327
Louison - v. Compagni, 2 - Tel. 293776
Lucca - v. Castaldi, 33 - Tel. 265708
Lucco M. - v. S. Vito, 5 - Tel. 807690
Lucia - v. Ravizza, 2 - Tel. 437872
Lupetta - v. Lupetta, 3 - Tel. 899257
Magni C. - v. Benef. dell'Ospedale Maggiore, 24 - Telefo-
    no 6427503
Malacalza G. - v. Pergolesi, 19 - Tel. 222678

Malatesta - v. B. di Savoia, 19 - Tel. 5461079
Mancini - v. Omboni, 4 - Tel. 276472
Marchi V. - v. Mora, 11 - Tel. 873050
Margutti M. - v. Stelvio, 51 - Tel. 673828
Marino - v. P. della Francesca, 38 - Tel. 344704
Merano - v. Palazzi, 24 - Tel. 265153
Metanopoli - v. Emilia, 2 - S. Donato Mil. - Tel. 510155
Mik Mak - v. Certosa, 134 - Tel. 305585
My Grill Principe e Savoia - p.za Repubblica, 17 - Tel. 6230
Mille Luci - v. Serra, 54 - Tel. 390360
Montecarlo - v. G. Galeazzo, 7 - Tel. 8375641
Montecatini - v. Ferruccio, 1 - Tel. 341304
Montecatini Alto - vl. Monza, 7 - Tel. 286773
Monteverdi - v. Monteverdi, 15 - Tel. 269091
Moroni & Pucci - v. Armorari, 8 - Tel. 890229
Motta - p.le Cadorna - Staz. Nord - Tel. 893171
Narducci G. - v. Broggi, 5 - Tel. 266885
Nencini - v. Tadino, 9 - Tel. 221409
Nocino - v. S. Gregorio, 11 - Tel. 266115
Okay - v. Bonvesin de la Riva, 9 - Tel. 745447 - 723497
Olivo - v. Principe Amedeo, 3 - Tel. 650682
Orologio - v. Speronari, 8 - Tel. 874474
O'Scugnizzo - vl. Cassala, 59 - Tel. 851161
Osteria Al Cancello Rosso - v. Tofane, 1 - Tel. 280387
Osteria del Vecchio Canneto - v. Solferino, 56 - Tel. 638498
Pam-Pam - v. S. Paolo, 15 - Tel. 892835
Paolina - v. Larga, 8 - Tel. 800889
Paradiso - v. Melzo, 21 - Tel. 279215
Parini « Da Giulio » - v. Parini, 7 - Tel. 665170
Planta Blanca - v. Corelli, 62 - Tel. 7385226
Piccadilly - v. Lodovico il Moro, 55 - Tel. 470741
Piccolo Padre - v. Bianca Maria, 2 - Tel. 798481
Pierett - v. Veniero, 2 - Tel. 368269
Pic Nic - v. Camperio, 1 - Tel. 806710
Pistoiese - v. Lazzaretto, 15 - Tel. 665983
Ponticello - v. Arimondi, 1 - Tel. 390863
Prospero - v. Corridoni, 10 - Tel. 701345
Quattro Lanterne - v. Savona, 17 - Tel. 8390017
Quattro Mori - v. Dante, 9 - Tel. 872208
Quattro Nazioni - v. Broletto, 18 - Tel. 875546
Rib Room (Hotel Hilton) - v. Galvani, 12 - Tel. 6983
Riccione - v. Taramelli, 70 - Tel. 683807
Rigolo - v. Solferino, 11 - Tel. 899768

Rigoletto - v. V. Monti, 33 - Tel. 893487
Ristorante Iraniano - v.le Bianca Maria, 8 - Tel. 700017
Ristorante La Pianta - Corsico - v. Cavour, 47 - Tel. 4471094
Ristorante Monterosa - p.le Lotto, 14 - Tel. 364093
Ristorante « Pinocchio » - v. Eustachi, 13 - Tel. 200082
Rizzo G. - v. Graziano, 35 - Tel. 6422025
Rogoredo - v. Cassinis, 76 - Tel. 530975
Roof. Garden Palace Hotel - p.za Repubblica, 20 - Tel. 6336
Romani B. - v. Trebazio, 2 - Tel. 340738
Romani M. - v. Zebedia, 9 - Tel. 807915
Romano - v. Plinio, 72 - Tel. 2363474
Rosy e Gabriele - v. Sirtori, 26 - Tel. 2041930
Rubicone - v. Capecelatro, 91 - Tel. 4031801
S. Carlo - p. Dergano, 1 - Tel. 690117
S. Lucia - v. S. Pietro all'Orto, 3 - Tel. 793155
San Maurilio - v. S. Maurilio, 17 - Tel. 875907
Samovar - v. Venezian, 14 - Tel. 2360214
Sampietro C. - p. XXV Aprile, 1 - Tel. 635815
Sangallo - v. Sangallo, 41 - Tel. 730286
Sardella G. - v. Puccini, 2 - Tel. 802284
S.A.R.F. - Stazione Porta Garibaldi - Tel. 661076
S.A.R.F. - Stazione p. IV Novembre - Tel. 671817
Sarni A. - v. Dante, 7 - Tel. 866436
Sassoscritto - c.so Magenta, 96 - Tel. 432531
Savini - gall. Vittorio Emanuele II - Tel. 898343
Self Service - v. S. Maria alla Porta, 2 - Tel. 866040
Sempione - v. Manuzio, 11 - Tel. 662715
Serafino - v. Bramante, 35 - Tel. 335363
Settebello - v. P. Castaldi, 17 - Tel. 279857
Settecupole - v. Ippolito Nievo, 33 - Tel. 341290
Splugen Brau - c. Europa, 12 - Tel. 709329
St. Andrews' - v. S. Andrea, 23 - Tel. 793132
Stagni Fratelli - v. Compagni, 2 - Tel. 293776
Stazione Centrale - p.za L. di Savoia, 1 - Tel. 273851
Stella d'Oro - v. Donizetti, 3 - Tel. 705580
Stella d'Oro - v. Spallanzani, 10 - Tel. 225952
Stomaco di Ferro - v. Osti, 4 - Tel. 877648
Su Nuraghe - v. Roncaglia, 3 - Tel. 431475
Taverna del Gran Sasso - pl. pr. Clotilde, 10 - Tel. 637578
Taverna del Grillo - v. Fabrizi, 2 - Tel. 3555152
Taverna della Giarrettiera - v. Pellico, 8 - Tel. 870697
Tavernetta - v. Fatebenefratelli, 30 - Tel. 637610
Tipico Giapponese Endo - v. Filzi, 8 - Tel. 635017

Tirreno - p. Duca d'Aosta, 12 - Tel. 222690
Tombolini - v. Lazzaretto, 15 - Tel. 665983
Toscana Adriana - v. Cola di Rienzo, 57 - Tel. 479420
Toscanino - p. Erculea, 9 - Tel. 873589
Toscano - v. Poerio, 3 - Tel. 795466
Toscano - v. S. Gerolamo Emiliani, 2 - Tel. 573954
Toscano al Chianti - v. Castaldi, 31 - Tel. 225010
Toscano ai Bastioni - vl. Pasubio, 8 - Tel. 635574
Toscano da Gori - v. Sammartini, 21 - Tel. 691607
Toscano « Da Ilia » - v. Lecco, 1/a - Tel. 273559
Toscano da Luigi (Gigi) - p. Risorgimento, 8 - Tel. 740745
Toscano da Mario - c.so Concordia, 10 - Tel. 780676
Toscano « Da Mario » - p. Beccaria, 12 - Tel. 802494
Toscano da Natalino - v. Monte Amiata, 4 - Tel. 430343
Toscano da Remo - l. Domodossola, 2 - Tel. 312003
Toscano da Ulisse - v. Palma, 26 - Tel. 4080238
Toscano da Vittorio - c. G. Garibaldi, 68 - Tel. 651511
Toscano Pace - v. Washington, 74 - Tel. 468567
Transatlantico - v. Malpighi, 3 - Tel. 221919
Trattoria al Soldato d'Italia - v. Fiori Chiari, 10 - Tel. 804409
Trattoria Calafuria - v. Castelvetro, 18 - Tel. 384704
Trattoria Cassina de' Pomm - v. Gioia, 194 - Tel. 691448
Trattoria da Giovanni - v. Mincio, 9 - Tel. 560486
Trattoria La Pesa - v. Morosini, 12 - Tel. 542906
Trattoria del Poulireu - v. Ripamonti, 337 - Tel. 530954
Trattoria della Gobba - v. Padova, 395 - Tel. 2560081
Trattoria La Sigala - v. Scipioni, 3 - Tel. 225704
Trattoria Tosc. da Fumino - v. Bernina, 43/45 - Tel. 606872
Trattoria Vecchie Abbadesse - v. Abbadesse, 20 - Tel. 691591
Tre Gobbi - v. Marghera, 3 - Tel. 432311
Tre Pini - v. T. Morgagni, 19 - Tel. 678464
Trietel D. - p. S. Maria Beltrade, 4 - Tel. 872702
Tubia A. - v. Renzo e Lucia, 5 - Tel. 8435796
Tulipan - v. Tadino, 2 - Tel. 276426
Union Ris - v. Unione, 8 - Tel. 866103
Valdarno - v. Modena, 28 - Tel. 716874
Vasco Fucecchio - v. Porpora, 161 - Tel. 230591
Vasco - v. Durini, 26 - Tel. 780727
Vecchia Ost. Laghetto - v. Festa d. Perdono, 1 - Tel. 793656
Vecchia Milano - v. G. Galeazzo, 25 - Tel. 8397365
Vecchia Parigi - v. Calabiana, 3 - Tel. 560594
Verdi - p. Mirabello, 5 - Tel. 651412
Versilia - v. A. Doria, 44 - Tel. 225187

Viareggio - v. A. Certosa, 36 - Tel. 365668
Victoria - p. Cinque Giornate, 6 - Tel. 588293
Vignetta - v. Valassina, 16 - Tel. 600579
Virdis - v. Bellotti, 4 - Tel. 705578
Vip - v. Hoepli, 6 - Tel. 898472
Wienerwald - gall. Vitt. Eman. - Tel. 870697

DANCINGS - NIGHT CLUBS

Apollo Danze - v. Procaccini, 17 - Tel. 312922
Astoria Club - p.za S. Maria Beltrade, 2 - Tel. 808787
Bang Bang - v. della Chiusa, 13 - Tel. 875879
Big Ben - v. Certosa, 85 - Tel. 391413
Bounty (The) - v. Baracchini, 13 - Tel. 896798
Buca D'Este - Rist. Taverna - v. Bligny, 23/a - Tel. 541777
Caffè Genzianella - v. Sarpi, 33 - Tel. 381290
Charlie Max - v. Marconi, 2 - Tel. 871416
Club Number 1 - v. Dell'Annunciata, 31 - Tel. 651203
El Marocco - Night Club - v. Baracchini, 1 - Tel. 866998
Embassy Club - v. S. Damiano, 3/a - Tel. 791226
Fitzgerald - c.so Europa, 5/7 - Tel. 709052
Gatto Verde - v. Scarlatti, 32 - Tel. 209515
Haway Night Club - v. Valvassori Peroni, 41 - Tel. 293539
Hi-Fi Club - p.za del Duomo - Tel. 866422
Jolly Club - v. S. Pietro All'Orto - Tel. 792730
La Porta d'oro - p. Diaz, 3 - Tel. 808541
Little Club - v. Bonnet, 11 - Tel. 653383
Maxim Dancing - v. Manzoni, 42 - Tel. 700528 - 794122
Meridiana (la) - v. Cellini, 2 - Tel. 702938
Moulin Rouge - Night Club - v. Durini, 25 - Tel. 793783
Montemerlo Dancing - Giardini Pubblici - Tel. 200604
Nepentha - p.za Diaz, 1 - Tel. 804837
Night Club « Caprice » - v. Borgogna, 5 - Tel. 793389
Night William's Club - l. Cairoli, 1 - Tel. 877218
Night Club « La Tour d'Orient » - v. Filzi, 41 - Tel. 6881483
Paips - c.so Europa, 9 - Tel. 799775
Petra Club - v.le Piceno, 3 - Tel. 714484 - 7384801
Pigalle - Galleria Buenos Aires, 33 - Tel. 265401
Punta dell'Est - Bar - Idroscalo Milano - Tel. 746067
Ragno d'Oro - p.le Medaglie d'Oro, 2 - Tel. 541406
Ravito de oro - gall. Passarella, 1 - Tel. 793595
7/40 CLUB - v. Carducci, 25 - Tel. 879597
Sexy Club - p. Pio XI, 5 - Tel. 871805
Sing Sing - v. Merlo, 3 - Tel. 780221

Tam-Tam Dancing -v. S. Gimignano, 10 - Tel. 4150067
Top Town Club - v. Baracchini, 7 - Tel. 806151
Trianon Dancing - c.so Vitt. Eman. II, 11 - Tel. 705945
Tricheco Club - v. Monza, 140 - Tel. 2575258
Zonno U. - v. Fabio Massimo, 35/61 - Tel. 560526
Wanted Saloon - v. Alemagna, 6 - Tel. 897081

AMERICAN BAR

Baretto Monkey - v. S. Andrea, 3 - Tel. 705031
Bar Mario - v. Montenapoleone, 1 - Tel. 701958
Ennio's Bar - p.za Diaz, 1 - Tel. 877490
Simon Bar - c.so Vercelli, 62 - Tel. 4692960

CABARET

Biberon - v. De Amicis, 13 - Tel. 720800
Cab - v. S. Sofia, 24
Derby Club - v. Monterosa, 84 - Tel. 430027 - 4691579
Settepiù Club - v. Astesani, 41 - Tel. 6463409

CAVES

Arethusa - v. Giardino, 1 - Tel. 890330
Escudero - v. S. Giovanni sul Muro, 4 - Tel. 861162
Giamaica - v. Brera, 26 - Tel. 876723
Saloon Tecla - v. S. Tecla, 3 - Tel. 896620 - 893203
Shanghai - v.le Col di Lana, 4 - Tel. 8483671

DANCING - NIGHT CLUB

For You Club - Gall. S. Babila, 4 - Tel. 782429
Good Mood - v. Turati, 29 - Tel. 669349
Mio Mao - v. Canonica, 32 - Tel. 384906
Rayito de Oro - v. Larga, 23 - Tel. 800.601 - 804.833
Silver Club - c.so P. Romana, 106/2 - Tel. 5462874
Taverna del Centro - p.za Duomo, 2 - Tel. 800129
Ferrario - p.za Duomo, 10 - Tel. 871129
Tequila - c.so Sempione, 65 - Tel. 339057
Taverna Lucky - v. T. Livio, 2 - Tel. 585983

WHISKY A GOGO'

A.B.C. Gogò - v. S. Michele D. Carso, 20 - Tel. 439640
Al Grouse - p.le Bonomelli, 5 - Tel. 5399028
Al Pick Up - v. Donatello, 37 - Tel. 2365082
Al Rififì - p.le Biancamano, 2 - Tel. 661532
Al Whisky Notte - p. C. Erba - v. Plinio, 63 - Tel. 2041482

Alla Lanterna - c.so Garibaldi, 68 - Tel. 661532
Alla Tarantola - v. Principe Eugenio, 15 - Tel. 344040
Covo Club - v. Pasubio, 3 - Tel. 652657
Lotito - c.so Sempione, 65 - Tel. 339057
Philippe Baba, p.za Segesta - Tel. 879021
Safari - v. Pasquirolo, 8 - Tel. 792558
Sphinx's - v. Papiniano, 59 - Tel. 835637
Tibi Dabo - v. Padova, 95 - Tel. 2896344

SPORTING GROUNDS, CLUBS AND ASSOCIATIONS

Arena Civica - v. Byron, 2 - Tel. 341924
Asahi Judo Club e Aikido - v. della Passione, 9 - Tel. 798759
Automobilismo - Autodromo al Parco di Monza - Pista rossa per Go-Kart all'Idroscalo
Automodellismo - Pista Automodelli - Autodromo di Monza
Bonacossa - v. Mecenate, 76 - Tel. 5061277
Bowling Corvetto - v. Marco d'Agrate, 23
Bowling dei fiori - Naviglio Pavese - Quartiere Torretta
Bowling Loreto - v. Cavezzali, 9
Bowling Cinisello - Cinisello Balsamo - v.le Romagna, 31
Cameroni - v. Bechi, 2 - Tel. 2576740
Campo Sportivo Ripamonti - v. Iseo, 4 - Tel. 6459253
Canottieri Milano - Nav. Grande, 160 - Tel. 479211
Canottieri Olona - Naviglio Grande, 146 - Tel. 479457
Cappelli - p.za Caduti del Lavoro, 5 - Tel. 830253
Cappelli-Sforza - v. Lampugnano, 80 - Tel. 303525
Centro Giovanile Card. Schuster - v. Feltre, 90 - Tel. 218924

Centro Ippico Lombardo - v. Fetonte, 21 - Tel. 4084270
Centro Kennedy - v. Olivieri, 15 - Tel. 4596783
Centro Mil. Sport e Ricreazione - p. Diaz, 1/a - Tel. 899158
Centro Sportivo Pirelli - v. Sarca, 202, Bicocca - Tel. 6222
Centro Univ. Sportivo Milano - p. da Vinci, 32 - Tel. 296391
Circolo Bocciofila Brianza - v. Aporti, 22 - Tel. 2893923
Circolo Culturale e Ricreativo all'Onestà - v. Procaccini 38 - Tel. 311472
Circolo Milan A.C. - p. S. Alessandro, 4 - Tel. 864390
Circolo Sportivo Inter - v. Amedei 2/a - Tel. 896289
Club Alpino Italiano - v. Foscolo, 3 - Tel. 897519
Club Amici Nerazzurri - v. Lanzone, 31 - Tel. 877232
Club Milanese Automotoveicoli d'Epoca - v. Cerva, 44 - Tel. 794236
Colombo - v. del Cardellino, 1 - Tel. 410972
C.O.N.I. - c.so Porta Vigentina, 54 - Tel. 593002
Conte Biacamano - Circonv. Idroscalo, 3 - Tel. 9060093
Corse al galoppo e al trotto - Ippodromi di San Siro (Piazzale dello Sport, 10) - Ippodromo di Mirabello (Parco di Monza)
Dopolavoro Ferroviario - Idroscalo - Tel. 7384486
Est Milano, Sporting Club - p. S. Stefano, 7 - Tel. 878140
F.A.L.C. - v. Disciplini, 2 - Tel. 893876
Federaz. Italiana della Caccia - v. S. Tecla, 5 - Tel. 800675
Federaz. Ital. Gioco Calcio - v. F. Casati, 33/a - Tel. 637770
Federaz. Italiana Gioco Calcio - Lega Naz. Professionisti - vl. Filippetti, 26/a - Tel. 5460651
Federaz. Ital. Motonautica - v. Cappuccio, 19 - Tel. 874410
Federaz. Italiana Pallacanestro - c.so Porta Vigentina, 54 - Tel. 5460329
Federaz. Italiana Pesca Sportiva - v. Gadio, 2 - Tel. 896549
Federaz. Italiana Rugby - v. Cerva, 30 - Tel. 781417
Federaz. Italiana Sci Nautico - v. Zuretti, 102 - Tel. 6086233
Federaz. Ital Sport Bocce - v. Boscovich, 50 - Tel. 270863
Federaz. Ital. Sport Equestri - c. Sempione, 73 - Tel. 316163
Federaz. Ital. Sport Invernali - v. Cerva, 30 - Tel. 705167
Federaz. Ital. Tennis - c. Porta Vigentina, 54 - Tel. 573502
Federaz. Medico Sportiva Italiana - vl. Repubblica Cisalpina, 3 - Tel. 339339
Federaz. Pugilistica Italiana - v. Dante, 16 - Tel. 870488
Forza e Coraggio - v. Gallura, 8 - Tel. 563130

Fossati - v. Cambini, 4 - Tel. 2826796
Galoppo - v. Caprilli, 30
Ginnastica Pro Patria - vl. Romagna, 18 - Tel. 723080
Giuriati - v. Pascal, 6 - Tel. 292358
Greppi Dajelli - v. Faenza, 7 - Tel. 810202
Gruppo Amici della Montagna - v. Merlo, 3 - Tel. 799178
Gruppo Cronisti Milanesi - v. Freguglia, 1 - Tel. 793248/
  794545 - v. della Moscova, 19 - Tel. 661510
Gruppo Sport. « Lombardina » - v. Brusuglio, 26 - Tel. 683057
  Presidente Franco Boccardi
Idroscalo - Gare di motonautica, canottaggio e sci nautico -
  (accesso da Viale E. Forlanini)
Imprese Sportive, v. Cantù, 2 - Tel. 876247
Internazionale Football Club - v. Dante, 7 - Tel. 892352
Ippodromo di San Siro - Segreteria della S.I.R.E. - Porta
  Romana, 3 - Tel. 873216
Iris 1914 - v.le Liguria, 50 - Tel. 845.020
Jigoro Kano Judo Club - v. Solari, 6 - Tel. 439608
Judo Club Universo - v. Crocefisso, 5 - Tel. 808872
Kodokan Judo Club - v. Battaglia, 27 - Tel. 2826273
Lega Ciclismo Professionistico - v. A. Paoli, 6 - Tel. 654702
Lido - p.le Lotto, 15 - Tel. 391679
Mangiarotti Circolo della Spada - v. Solferino, 24 - Tel.
  661188
Marchese Cerva - v. Colleoni - Tel. 347082
Mauro - v. Ussi, 18 - Tel. 6435564
Milan Associazione Calcio - v. Turati, 3 - Tel. 669016
Minigolf Riviera di Milano (Idroscalo)
Moto Club Milano - v. Washington, 33 - Tel. 437110
Motonautica - v. Anfossi, 32 - Tel. 581812
Naz. Atleti Azzurri d'Italia - v. Foscolo, 3 - Tel. 867209
Naz. Uff. Gara Ciclismo - v. Ausonio, 27 - Tel. 851051
Niguarda - v. Ornato, 90/100 - Tel. 6429534
Nuoto Club di Milano - vl. Tunisia, 40 - 666327
Nuovo Giuriati - v. Valv. Peroni, 48 - Tel. 2366254
Palazzo dello sport - p.le 6 Febbraio
Palazzo Lido Sport - p. Stuparich, 1 - Tel. 391667
Palazzo del Ghiaccio - v. Piranesi, 14 - Tel. 726097
Pallacanestro Simmenthal - v. Caltanissetta, 3 - Tel. 723711
Pavesi - v. De Lemene, 3 - Tel. 395190
Polisportiva Libertas - v. Fabio Massimo, 1 - Tel. 537328
Polo Club - Parco di Monza
Pugilato - v.le Bligny, 52

Rari-Nantes Milano - pl. Cadorna, 4 - Tel. 800888
Rugby: Campo sport. Giuriati - v. Pascal, 6 - Tel. 232358
   Centro Polisportivo - v. Valvassori P., 48
S.A.I. - c. Porta Romana, 122 - Tel. 558032
Scuola Ippica al Parco di Monza
Sferisterio Milano - v. Palermo, 10 - Tel. 896250
Società Trenno - c. Porta Romana, 3/c - Tel. 804541
Solbiatese - v. Gulli, 29 - Tel. 4076859
Sport Club Fratelli Zanazzi - v. Dezza, 43 - Tel. 437859
Sporting Club il Sole - v. Paolo da Cannobio, 5 - Tel. 890438
Sportiva Aldo & Vanni Borletti - v. Costanza, 21 - Tel. 482657
Sportivo Circolo Milano 1905 - v. Maddalena, 4 - Tel. 876906
Stadio S. Siro - v. dei Piccolomini, 5 - Tel. 4084123
Tennis Club Ambrosiano - v. Feltre, 33 - Tel. 218917
Tennis Club Domus - v. Taccioli, 27 - Tel. 6450988
Tennis Club Lombardo - v. Sismondi, 8 - Tel. 717231
Tennis Club Milano - v. Arimondi, 15 - Tel. 394194
Tennis Junior - v. Cavriana, 45 - Tel. 7388222
Tiro a Segno Nazionale - p. Accursio, 21 - Tel. 391418
Tiro a volo (piattello, piccione, skeet) - v. Macconago, 36
   - Tel. 5394037
Trotto Italiano - p. Duca d'Aosta, 8/b - Tel. 270900
Trotto Sportsman - p. Duca d'Aosta, 8/b - Tel. 270004
U.C.I.P. - c.so Porta Vigentina, 54 - Tel. 553740
Unione Ital. Sport Popolare - Porta Vittoria, 43 - Tel. 706715
Unione Naz. Veterani Sportivi - v. Foscolo, 3 - Tel. 872567
U.R.I. - v. Stradella, 5 - Tel. 279847
Velodromo Vigorelli - v. Arona, 19 - Tel. 381513
XXV Aprile - v. Cimabue, 24 - Tel. 322689
Vespa Club d'Italia - v. Trebazio, 5 - Tel. 389723
Volo a vela - Aeroporto di Bresso

PISCINE COMUNALI COPERTE

Cozzi - v. Tunisia, 35 - Tel. 639703
Mincio - v. Mincio, 13 - Tel. 538416
Parco Solari - v. Montevideo, 11 - Tel. 4695278

PISCINE COMUNALI SCOPERTE

Argelati - v. Segantini, 6 - Tel. 8480012
Caimi - v. Botta, 18 - Tel. 554754
Cambini - v. Cambini, 6 - Tel. 2820544
Lido - p. Lotto, 15 - Tel. 366100

TAXIS

Alla partenza il prezzo è di L. 220 comprensivo del 1º scatto di m. 220. Per scatti successivi L. 40 per ogni m. 400. Prezzo di fermo da L. 1.200 a L. 1.800 per ora (pari a L. 40 per ogni 80 secondi). Supplemento festivo (domenica e festività dalle 6 alle 22) L. 100 per corsa e non cumulabile col supplemento notturno. Supplemento notturno (per tutti i giorni dalle 22 alle 6) da L. 150 a L. 200.

Valigie e bagagli - Ciascun collo successivo al primo avente il lato superiore a cm. 50, L. 50.

Sci - Ciascun paio di sci L. 100.

Cani - Per ciascun cane, esclusi quelli da grembo, L. 50.

AUTORADIOTASSI

Servizio chiamata autopubbliche mediante radiotelefono 866151/865161

ZONA AFFORI - Niguarda

v.le Affori, ang. v. Astesani - Tel. 6456713
vl. F. Testi, ang. v. Pianell - Tel. 6431432
p. Gasparri - Tel. 6462380
v. Hermada, ang. v. Ornato - Tel. 6431595

ZONA CENTRO

Lg. Augusto - Tel. 700148
p. s. Babila (c. Matteotti) - Tel. 702719
Lg. Carrobbio - Tel. 867605
v. Croce Rossa - Tel. 654975
P.za Duomo ang. v. Mazzini - Tel. 872693
p. della Scala - Tel. 872662
p. Fontana - Tel. 867647
v. Gonzaga - Tel. 8676649
v. Puccini ang. Foro Bonaparte - Tel. 873028
v. S. Eufemia ang. c. Italia - Tel. 867370

ZONA CITTA' STUDI - LAMBRATE

p. Ascoli - Tel. 276887
v. Beato Angelico ang. v. Sangallo - Tel. 726780
p. Bottini - staz. Lambrate - Tel. 2364375
v. Palmanova ang. v. Cesana - Tel. 2850674
vl. Romagna ang. P. Piola - Tel. 235670
v. Teodosio ang. v. Porpora - Tel. 235680

ZONA GARIBALDI - PORTA NUOVA - VOLTA

Lg. Treves - Tel. 662960
p. XXV Aprile - Tel. 662349
v. Cagliero ang. v. Stefini - Tel. 600395
p. Cavour ang. v. Manin - Tel. 666721
p. Dergano ang. v. Brivio - Tel. 6085910
v. Farini - Tel. 6086555
pl. Istria - Tel. 603879
pl. Lagosta - Tel. 6881856
v. Mercato ang. v. Tivoli - Tel. 861104
p. della Repubblica - Tel. 662152
v. Vincenzo da Seregno - Tel. 6459562

ZONA GRECO - TURRO - CRESCENZAGO

vl. Monza ang. v. S. Erlembardo - Tel. 2575201
Via Oxilia ang. Morbegno - Tel. 2895795
v. Padova ang. v. Cambini - Tel. 2850517
v. Padova ang. v. Giulietti - Tel. 2561152
p. Precotto - Tel. 2576013
vl. Rimembranze di Greco - Tel. 6881850
v. Rovereto - Tel. 2893777
p. S. Francesca Romana - Tel. 272736

ZONA MAGENTA - S. SIRO

p. Amendola - Tel. 483616
p. Axum - Tel. 4076547
pl. Baracca - Tel. 495415
v. Bellini - ang. p. Frattini - Tel. 4225674
vl. Cassiodoro ang. v. G. Rossetti - Tel. 4695121
p. De Angeli ang. v. Faruffini - Tel. 4696785
v. Forze Armate ang. v. Cabella - Tel. 4594812
pl. Giovanni dalle Bande Nere - Tel. 4076442
pl. Lotto - Tel. 4695119
p. Melozzo da Forlì - Tel. 4071574
p. Monte Falterona - Tel. 4087054
p. Napoli ang. v. Solari - Tel. 470802

p. Piemonte - Tel. 430322
v. Saint Bon ang. v. Forze Armate - Tel. 4076445
p. S. Ambrogio - Tel. 867374
p. Siena ang. v. Padulli - Tel. 4070838
p. Tripoli - Tel. 4225300
p. Virgilio - Tel. 867603

ZONA MONFORTE - VENEZIA

p. Argentina - Tel. 2041501
c. Buenos Aires ang. p. Lima - Tel. 276770
pl. Dateo - Tel. 723536
pl. Loreto ang. v. Costa - Tel. 280135
p. Oberdan - Tel. 206533
p. Tricolore - Tel. 798535

ZONA SEMPIONE - BOVISA

pl. Accursio ang. v. Papa - Tel. 394390
v. Antona Traversi - Tel. 3553130
pl. Bausan - Tel. 370890
p. Castelli Pompeo - Tel. 394385
v. Ceresio - Tel. 335415
pl. Cimitero Maggiore - Tel. 304789
p. Diocleziano - Tel. 313419
v. Drago ang. lg. Boccioni - Tel. 3555002
p. Firenze - Tel. 390388
p. Gramsci - Tel. 342020
p. Lega Lombarda ang. v. Bramante - Tel. 313616
p. Nigra - Tel. 373233
p. Prealpi - Tel. 395892
p. Sempione - Tel. 342132
c. Sempione ang. v. Domodossola - Tel. 335976

ZONA STAZIONE CENTRALE

p. Cincinnato - Tel. 667351
v. Ponte Seveso ang. vl. Lunigiana - Tel. 680215
pl. Stazione Centrale - Tel. 222786

ZONA TICINESE - GENOVA - GIAMBELLINO

p. Abbiategrasso - Tel. 8435590
v. De Amicis ang. Conca del Naviglio - Tel. 8391221
v. Dei Missaglia - Tel. 8262190
v. Fra' Cristoforo (Quartiere Torretta) - Tel. 8493945
p. Miani - Tel. 817410
p. Negrelli (Ang. v. L. il Moro) - Tel. 4225676

v. Solari ang. vl. Coni Zugna - Tel. 8480047
v. Torricelli ang. v. Meda - Tel. 851473
p. Tirana ang. v. Inganni - Tel. 4155804
pl. XXIV Maggio - Tel. 8486575

ZONA VITTORIA - ROMANA - VIGENTINA

v. Bergamo ang. vl. Montenero - Tel. 581007
p. Bonomelli ang. v. Brenta - Tel. 5399184
v. Cassinis - stazione Rogoredo - Tel. 564906
p. Card. Ferrari - Tel. 545106
p. Cinque Giornate - Tel. 573422
vl. Corsica ang. v. Negroli - Tel. 718253
p. Corvetto - Tel. 564445
p. Emilia - Tel. 742426
v. Faà di Bruno ang. p.za Cuoco - Tel. 585851
c. Lodi ang. p. Lodi - Tel. 545092
c. Lodi ang. p. Medaglie d'Oro - Tel. 573410
vl. Mugello ang. vl. Corsica - Tel. 723747
p. Ovidio - Tel. 718255
pl. Porta Lodovica - Tel. 850998
c. Porta Romana ang. c. Vigentina - Tel. 581019
v. Ripamonti ang. v. Noto - Tel. 5394737
v. Ripamonti ang. v. Serio - Tel. 5399121
vl Ungheria - Tel. 503435

A.C.I.
(AUTOMOBIL CLUB ITALIANO OFFICES)

Automobile Club Milano - C.so Venezia, 43 - Tel. 7745

Centri di assistenza tecnica: v. Silva, 10 - lavaggio - lubrificaz., Tel. 4696267 - diagnosi, Tel. 4696247 - cessione auto, Tel. 4696339 - SSS, Tel. 4696333
v.le Ortles, 81 - lavaggio - lubrificaz., Tel. 5397046 - diagnosi, Tel. 5397047 - cessione auto, Tel. 5397048
v. Pola, 9 - lavaggio rapido - lubrificaz., Tel. 6886041

MILANO

p.le Bacone (ang. v. Ozanam) - Tel. 279410
v. Cabella, 2 - Tel. 4562124
v.le Coni Zugna, 37 - Tel. 437852
v. Varese, 20 - Tel. 637408
v. Palmanova, 75 - Tel. 2825956
p.le Maciachini, 10 - Tel. 677584

v. Cassinis, 55 - Tel. 560288
c.so Sempione, 41 - Tel. 316513
v.le Sabotino, 19 - Tel. 585621
v.le Romagna, 10 - Tel. 7384571/572
v. d'Alviano, 1 - Tel. 4229244
v.le Sarca, 189 - Tel. 6432142
v. Fantoli, 10 - Tel. 5060383

PROVINCIA DI MILANO

Abbiategrasso - c.so San Martino, 55 - Tel. 942478
Arcore - v. Casati, 143 - Tel. 64240
Besana Brianza - v. Provinciale, 30 - Tel. 94143
Binasco - c.so Matteotti, 3 - Tel. 9055320
Bollate - Fraz. Ospiate - v. Trento, 12 - Tel. 9902918
Cassano d'Adda - v. Manzoni, 14 - Tel. 6137
Castano Primo - v. M. Tadini, 22 - Tel. 87458
Cesano Maderno - c.so Libertà (ang. v. S. Martino) - Tel. 51961
Cinisello Balsamo - v. Libertà - Tel. 9288916
Codogno - p.za XX Settembre, 7 - Tel. 32418
Corsico - v. Vitt. Emanuele, 18 - Tel. 4471104
Cusano Milanino - v. Valassina, ang. v. Pedretti - Tel. 9296436
Desio - v. G. Garibaldi, 162 - Tel. 66861
Gorgonzola - v. Italia, 71 - Tel. 950156
Legnano - c.so Sempione, 83 - Tel. 48530
Lissone - v. Matteotti, 29 - Tel. 42422
Lodi - c.so Mazzini, 2 - Tel. 52503
Magenta - v. Mazzini, 12/14 - Tel. 972289
Melegnano - v. Emilia, 63 - Tel. 980526
Melzo - p.za Vittorio Emanuele - Tel. 9550510
Monza - C.so Milano - Tel. 22388
Rho - v. Sempione, 75 - Tel. 9302300
S. Angelo Lodigiano - p. Libertà, 22 - Tel. 90480
Seregno - c.so Matteotti, 107 - Tel. 21605
Sesto San Giovanni - v. Don Minzoni, 132 - Tel. 2472577
Trezzo sull'Adda - v. Mazzini, 14 - Tel. 9090159
Vimercate - v. C. Battisti, 8 - Tel. 62650

UNIVERSITIES

Cattolica del Sacro Cuore - l.go Gemelli, 1 - Tel. 865551
Cattolica S. Cuore Augustinianum - v.le G. da Cermenate,
89/1 - Tel. 8463707
Commerciale L. Bocconi - v. Sarfatti, 25 - Tel. 830131
Degli Studi (Cliniche - Istituti) - v. Festa del Perdono, 7
Tel. 864341

Facoltà di Giurisprudenza - Scienze Politiche - Lettere e
Filosofia - Medicina e Chirurgia - Umanistiche - Scienze
Matematiche Fisiche e Naturali - v. Celoria, 22 - Tel.
2366596
Facoltà di Farmacia - v. Celoria, 22 - Tel. 2366348
Facoltà di Agraria e Medicina Veterinaria - via Celoria, 22
Tel. 2366492
Facoltà Scientifiche - v. Celoria, 22 - Tel. 2366573
Facoltà Umanistiche - p.za Missori, 4 - Tel. 866022
Interfacoltà - v. Festa del Perdono, 3 - Tel. 862507
Medicina Preventiva - v. Festa del Perdono, 3 - Tel. 862793
Centro di Cibernetica e di Attività linguistiche - v. Dave-
rio, 7 - Tel. 541519
Gruppo di Ricerca CNR - v. S. Antonio Zaccaria, 1 - Tel.
791354

MEDICINA E CHIRURGIA

Cattedra di Idrologia Medica - v. Vanvitelli, 32 - Tel. 717614
Chirurgica Generale I - v. F. Sforza, 35 - Tel. 542401
Chirurgica Generale II - v. Lamarmora, 11 - Tel. 541502
Delle Malattie Nervose e Mentali - v. F. Sforza, 35 - Tel.
585553
Dermosifilopatica - v. della Pace, 9 - Tel. 541325
Medica Generale - v. Sforza, 35 - Tel. 541593
Centro Cardioreumatologico - p.za C. Ferrari, 1 - Tel. 589880
Oculistica - v. della Commenda, 16 - Tel. 542448
Odontoiatrica - v. della Commenda, 10 - Tel. 584741
Ostetrica e Ginecologica - v. della Commenda, 12 - Tel.
593341
Otorinolaringoiatrica - v. della Commenda, 16 - Tel. 542463
Pediatrica - v. della Commenda, 9 - Tel. 544541
Anatomia Chirurgica e Corso di Operazioni - c.so di P.ta
Nuova, 23 - Tel. 638966
Anatomia e Istologia Patologica - v. F. Sforza, 38 - Tel.
874214
Anatomia Umana Normale - v. L. Mangiagalli, 31 - Tel.
292781
Biologia e Zoologia Generale e Centro di Studi di Genetica
Umana - v.so Venezia, 55 - Tel. 701167
Chimica Biologica - v. della Commenda, 19 - Tel. 585605
Chirurgia Plastica Ricostruttiva - v. della Commenda, 19
Tel. 598442
Farmacologia - v. Vanvitelli, 32 - Tel. 708220
Fisiologia Umana - v. L. Mangiagalli, 32 - Tel. 235474

Igiene - v. F. Sforza, 35 - Tel. 541937
Istologia ed Embriologia Generale - v. Ponzio, 7 - Tel. 292962
Malattie Infettive - v. Livigno, 3 - Tel. 690012
Medicina del Lavoro - v. S. Barnaba, 8 - Tel. 576091
Medicina Legale e delle Assicurazioni - v. L. Mangiagalli, 37
    - Tel. 292871
Microbiologia - v. L. Mangiagalli, 31 - Tel. 292556
Neurochirurgia - v. F. Sforza, 35 - Tel. 559158
Patologia Generale - v. L. Mangiagalli, 31 - Tel. 292515
Patologia Speciale Chirurgica - p.za Ospedale Maggiore, 3
    - Tel. 6444
Patologia Speciale Medica e Metodologia Clinica I - v. F.
    Sforza, 35 - Tel. 541744
Psichiatria - v. G. F. Besta, 1 (Affori) - Tel. 6453167
Psicologia - v. F. Sforza, 23 - Tel. 702759
Radiologia - p.za Gorini, 22 - Tel. 292176
Semeiotica Medica - v. F. Sforza, 35 - Tel. 542585
Biometria e Statistica Medica - v. Venezian, 1 - Tel. 292908
Storia della Medicina - v. Festa del Perdono, 3 - Tel. 899286
Tisiologia - v. F. Sforza, 35 - Tel. 553793
Urologia - v. della Commenda, 15 - Tel. 553766
Scuola di Perfezionamento in Cardiologia - v. F. Sforza,
    35 - Tel. 584342
Scuola per Tecnici di Istituti Medico-Biologici, - v. Celoria,
    10 - Tel. 292695

FARMACIA

Istituto di Farmacologia e Farmacognosia - v. Andrea del
    Sarto, 21 - Tel. 723066

SCIENZE MATEMATICHE FISICHE E NATURALI

Astronomia e Geodesia - v. Brera, 28 - Tel. 874444
Chimica Fisica - v. Saldini, 50 - Tel. 2365533
Chimica Generale ed Inorganica - v. Venezian, 21 - Tel.
    235427
Chimica Industriale - v. Saldini, 50 - Tel. 296352
Chimica Organica, 50 - v. Saldini, 50 - Tel. 293079
Elettrochimica e Metallurgia - v. Venezian, 21 - Tel. 235446
Fisiologia Generale - v. L. Mangiagalli, 32 - Tel. 235474
Genetica - v. Celoria, 10 - Tel. 230823
Geologia - p.za Gorini, 15 - Tel. 230328
Mineralogia Petrografia e Geochimica - v. Botticelli, 23 -
    Tel. 293994
Paleontologia - p.za Gorini, 15 - Tel. 230328
Scienze Botaniche - v. G. Colombo, 60 - Tel. 292161

Scienze Fisiche - v. Celoria, 16 - Tel. 2365541
Matematica - v. Saldini, 50 - 292393
Zoologia - v. Celoria, 10 - Tel. 2366364
Cattedra di Farmacologia - v. Vanvitelli, 32 - Tel. 7385568
Cattedra di Fisica Terrestre - v. Bonardi, 15 - Tel. 296707
Seminario Matematico e Fisico - p.za Leonardo da Vinci, 32
  - Tel. 2366163

AGRARIA - v. Celoria, 2

Agronomia Generale e Coltivazioni Erbacee - Tel. 292164
Anatomia e Fisiologia degli animali domestici - Tel. 296492
Biochimica Generale - Tel. 293662
Chimica Agraria - Tel. 230856
Chimica Organica - Tel. 292173
Coltivazioni Arboree - Tel. 292165
Economia e Politica Agraria - Tel. 292455
Entomologia Agraria - Tel. 2362880
Idraulica Agraria - Tel. 230512
Industrie Agrarie - Tel. 2365426
Microbiologia Industriale - Tel. 2367285
Microbiologia Agraria Tecnica - Tel. 230829
Patologia Vegetale - Tel. 296081
Zootecnica Generale - Tel. 292159

MEDICINA VETERINARIA - v. Celoria, 10

Anatomia degli animali domestici - Tel. 230920
Anatomia Patologica Veterinaria - Tel. 298225
Farmacologia - Tel. 2361178
Fisiologia della Nutrizione Animale - Tel. 292151
Ispezione degli Alimenti di Origine Animale - Tel. 2361528
Malattie Infettive Profilassi e Polizia Veterinaria - Tel.
  2366475
Medicina Legale Veterinaria - Tel. 2362724
Microbiologia ed Immunologia - Tel. 2361521
Ostetricia e Ginecologia Veterinaria - Tel. 292154
Parassitologia - Tel. 298325
Patologia Aviare - Tel. 298225
Patologia Generale Veterinaria - Tel. 298325
Patologia Speciale e Clinica Chirurgica Veterinaria - Tel.
  292157
Patologia Speciale e Clinica Medica Veterinaria - Tel. 292155
Radiologia Veterinaria - Tel. 235930
Zootecnica Generale Veterinaria - Tel. 293649
Centro Mastiti Bovine del C.N.R. - Tel. 235338
Internazionale degli Studi Sociali - p. Liberty, 4 - Tel. 700382
Popolare di Milano - p.za S. Alessandro, 4 - Tel. 896612

CONTENTS

Itineraries . . . . . page 3
A historical outline of Milan . . . » 7
The Cathedral . . . . » 10
The Cathedral square and the Royal Palace . » 18
The "Vittorio Emanuele" gallery . . » 20
Piazza Mercanti - Palazzo della Ragione -
    Loggia degli Osii . . . » 26
The Scala Theatre and square . . » 28
The square and the church of St. Fedele . » 34
The "Casa degli Omenoni" - Manzoni's
    house - The Poldi Pezzoli Museum . » 36
The basilica of St. Carlo . . . » 38
The church of St. Babila - The Seminario
    Maggiore . . . . » 40
The public gardens - The Natural History
    Museum - The Planetary . . . » 42
Villa Reale and the Modern Art Gallery . » 44
The Brera Picture-Gallery . . . » 46
St. Mark's Church . . . . » 50
St. Simpliciano's Basilica Virginum . » 52
The Sforzesco Castle and its art collections » 54
The Monumental Cemetery . . . » 64
The Arch of Peace or of Semplon . . » 66
The church of Santa Maria delle Grazie . » 70
Da Vinci's "Last Supper" . . . » 74
The Museum of Science and Technology . » 76
The Basilica of St. Ambrogio . . » 78
San Maurizio al Monastero Maggiore - The
    Archeological Museum - Palazzo Litta . » 84
The Ambrosian Library and its Art Gallery » 86
Santa Maria presso San Satiro . . » 88
St. Alexander's Church - The Arcimbolde
    Schools - The Trivulzio Building . » 90
The Basilica of St. Lorenzo Maggiore . » 92
St. Eustorgio and the Portinari Chapel . » 96
The Sanctuary of St. Maria and the church
    of St. Celso . . . . » 98
St. Nazaro in Brolo's . . . » 100
The Main Hospital . . . . » 102
S. Maria Della Passione's . . . » 106
St. Maria alla Fontana . . . » 107
The Charterhouse of Garegnano . . » 108
The Abbey of Chiaravalle Milanese . . » 110
The Vidoldone Abbey . . . » 114

The Abbey of Mirasole . . . . page 115
The Charterhouse of Pavia . . . » 117
Academies . . . . . . » 120
A.C.I. (Automobil Club Italiano offices) . » 185
Airports . . . . » 120
Ambulances . . . . . . » 129
Banks . . . . » 136
Boarding houses . . . . . » 157
Campings and youth hostels . . . » 134
Chambers of commerce . . . » 132
Charitable institutions . . . . » 130
Chemist's shops (open day and night) . » 147
Cinemas, Theatres . . . . » 135
Clinics . . . . » 138
Consulates . . . . . . » 143
Dancings . . . . . . » 177
Day-clinics . . . . . . » 161
Emergency addresses . . . . » 165
First aid . . . . . . » 164
Hotels . . . . » 123
Motels . . . . » 155
Museums, picture-galleries, libraries, art
    galleries . . . . . » 151
Night clubs . . . . . » 176
Parks and garden . . . . » 157
Policemen . . . . . . » 166
Police-stations . . . . . » 166
Postal and telegraph services . . » 161
Postal codes - Kilometre distances . » 141
Prefecture . . . . . . » 164
Railways . . . . . . » 148
Restaurants . . . . . » 167
Shipping and airways companies . . » 142
Sporting grounds, clubs and associations . » 178
Taxis . . . . » 182
Tourist organizations . . . . » 145
Town Hall . . . . . . » 155
Travelling agencies . . . . » 120
Universities . . . . . . » 186